# U N K N O W N
# CAPOEIRA

## VOLUME TWO

Also by Mestre Ricardo Cachorro

*Unknown Capoeira:*
*Secret Techniques of the Original Brazilian Martial Art*

# UNKNOWN
# CAPOEIRA

## VOLUME TWO

## A HISTORY OF THE
## BRAZILIAN MARTIAL ART

### Mestre Ricardo Cachorro

BLUE SNAKE BOOKS
BERKELEY, CALIFORNIA

Dekel Publishing House

Dekel Publishing House
P.O. Box 45094; Tel Aviv 61450, Israel
www.dekelpublishing.com
978-965-7178-15-7

Published in North America by Blue Snake Books
an imprint of North Atlantic Books
P.O. Box 12327, Berkeley, California 94712

*Cover and book design: Gisella Narcisi*  *English-language editing: Katie Roman*
*Cover photo: Ronald Smets\**  *Proofreading: Ilay Sofer*
*Cover photo background: João Barcelos*  *IPA terms: Dr. Maria Carmelita Padua Dias*

*Courtesy of Mestre Vladimir Frama. Copyright photo Ronald Smets (2000). Athletes: Mestre Vladimir Frama & Sunil "Indiano"—Batuque Capoeira Holland, www.capoeiraholland.com.

Printed in Israel

*Unknown Capoeira, Volume Two: A History of the Brazilian Martial Art* is sponsored by the Society for the Study of Native Arts and Sciences, a nonprofit educational corporation whose goals are to develop an educational and cross-cultural perspective linking various scientific, social, and artistic fields; to nurture a holistic view of arts, sciences, humanities, and healing; and to publish and distribute literature on the relationship of mind, body, and nature.

North Atlantic Books' publications are available through most bookstores. For further information, call 800-733-3000 or visit our websites at www.northatlanticbooks.com and www.bluesnakebooks.com.

New ISBN for Volume Two: 978-1-58394-234-5
Library of Congress Cataloging-in-Publication Data

Cachorro, Ricardo.
  Unknown Capoeira: secret techniques of the original Brazilian martial art / Ricardo Cachorro.
    p. cm.
  ISBN 978-1-58394-231-4 — ISBN 978-965-7178-14-0
  1. Capoeira (Dance) I. Title.
   GV1796.C145C24 2009
   793.3'1981—dc22

1 2 3 4 5 6 7 8 9 Dekel Productions, Tel Aviv 17 16 15 14 13 12

*To my Mestre, Adilson Camisa Preta,
and his Mestre, Roque*

*To those who came from far,
captive, and nevertheless
enriched in so many ways
the future of the world*

# ACKNOWLEDGMENTS

I am grateful to many people for making this book possible.

First, I would like to thank Prof. Geraldo Cesar Barbosa, Mestres Siqueira, Peixinho, Gato and Camisa for their support of the *Unknown Capoeira* project. The opinions expressed here are solely mine; however, their inspiration and generosity will never be forgotten.

My thanks also go to Mestre Vladimir Frama, to North Atlantic Books, to my friends Zvi Morik, publisher at Dekel Publishing House, and Hugo Gerstl, my new literary inspiration.

I am grateful to the people and institutions who have kindly given permission to reproduce material originally published or owned by them – and to everyone who was directly or indirectly involved in the production aspects of this book.

I would also like to thank my family for their love and support.

Finally, I have known great *capoeiristas*, some of whom became my friends. This book is indiscriminately dedicated to all of them.

**Mestre Ricardo Cachorro**
**Rio de Janeiro, July 2012**

# TABLE OF CONTENTS

# PREFACE

This book was written in response to the need for an up-to-date view of the origins of capoeira, and should be seen as a contribution to its amazing history – as a basis for new discussion, and not as a form of dogmatism.

Through new evidence and fresh interpretation, this work argues that capoeira did have its roots in Africa and African traditions before taking its final form in Brazil at two different historical moments. Other approaches and interpretations, most of which revolve around a specific ethnic group or geopolitical region, are an ongoing matter of debate among historians and capoeira fans worldwide. However, I believe that greater depth of understanding than that which arises from reading one book – or simply accepting culturally convenient, but scientifically dubious "facts" – is necessary to shed more light on this fascinating subject.

Regardless of one's historical or technical view, Capoeira Angola, Capoeira Regional, or "Capoeira Contemporânea" may have different spices, but, in the end, they are all just "capoeira" in the hearts and minds of the great *mestres*.

# INTRODUCTION

The main purpose of this book is to tell a story, one about the beautiful and intriguing history of capoeira, the Brazilian martial art, the fighting-game known by some as "dance-fight," that attracts people from all genders and age groups worldwide.

Many good books have been written about the history of capoeira. I read some and learned to respect them all. However, none of them, so far, have described its origins from an ethnic and cultural point of view, where evidence, sometimes subtle, sometimes crystal clear – whether transformed into hypotheses or found as facts – takes us far away from the usual beliefs, perhaps as far as thousands of miles from our old historical perceptions.

Nevertheless, to tell such a story, one needs to dare to have a bit of courage in order to dive into the thousands of pages and images, contemporary and (mostly) old, to come up with a different idea – both from a geographic and ethnic perspective – and arrive at an astonishing, surprisingly new adventure in the history of capoeira.

With these words, I must say, and apologize for the fact, that it was never my intention to comprehensively cover the Atlantic slave trade and the complex subject of African ethnicities in the New World. These are extensively covered by excellent books, old as well as new.

Having said that, I also must say that I did try my best to bring what I believe is new and relevant information concerning the specific ethnic groups

1

that introduced their cultural expressions to the colonial Americas, notedly Brazil, ultimately leading to the development of capoeira in Brazilian lands.

The first chapter, "First Came 12 Ships," tells the saga of the Akindele family, Yorùbá princes and princesses who came from Africa in the lost ship *Santa Maria do Cabo* during the early sixteenth century to work as slaves in Bahia, northeast Brazil. Prince Akindele becomes a king of his African homeland while still in chains in a strange land that he struggled to understand.

The second chapter, "Lords of the Atlantic," explores the great navigations that culminated in the Atlantic slave trade and the export of over twelve million African people from several different ethnic groups and locations to serve as slaves in the New World. Basic, relevant information is presented on the Portuguese, Spanish, English-British, French, Dutch, Danish–Norwegian, American and Swedish slave trade periods and achievements that influenced the new African cultures in the Americas.

In "The Cradle of Capoeira," the blending of cultures and ethnic groups, and the actual African peoples who brought the seeds of capoeira from Africa to the Caribbean and to Brazil are explained in their different – yet culturally linked – contexts. Slave revolts, the *quilombos*, the African dances, the N'Golo theory of Angola, the *Ag'ya* of Martinique, the creolized cultures and syncretic religions, the Adja-Yorùbá and Bantu influences in the birth of capoeira – myths and facts about the provenance of capoeira – are all discussed here.

The next chapter, "The Rise of Capoeira," explains how art played an important role for capoeira, from the simple analysis of a few of the most famous watercolors and works of the early nineteenth- and twentieth-century artists. An anthropological approach to the scenes depicted offers a consistent interpretation of the facts being "narrated" by each artist in a rich kaleidoscope of perspectives for the reader-*capoeirista* to think about – and analyze. Here, last but not least, the book pays homage to the modern founders of capoeira and to the capoeira schools that, based on a scale of worldwide popularity, contributed to the rise of capoeira in the twentieth and twenty-first centuries.

This chapter also touches on what could be considered the "missing link" between the Bahian capoeira of the nineteenth century and the capoeira that was developed in Rio de Janeiro in the 1960s. Here I offer a much deserved apology to the schools and *mestres* who could not be mentioned.

The last pages bring a list of capoeira moves and their international phonology based on the IPA (International Phonetic Alphabet), plus a glossary of the Yorùbá words used in the first chapter and a bibliography of the great works I had the pleasure to read during my research for this book. Thank you for reading it.

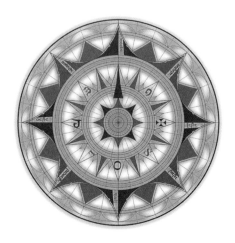

# First Came 12 Ships

Abimbola Akindele was a restless young man. At least for several of his last weeks at the *senzala* he worked as hard as he could to set an example for his family and his people. Abimbola was strong and determined. He knew he had to follow his ancestors' beliefs, and that he was being prepared for a great mission.

Four years earlier, in 1531, on the coast of recently "discovered" Brazil, he had survived the terrible journey on the *Santa Maria do Cabo*, a slave ship which sailed the Atlantic with more than 400 natives of Africa. These people had been literally piled up at the slave emporiums of the islands of Cape Verde, off the coast of Africa, where black natives from the recently contacted Bight of Benin were gathered before being shipped to Brazil as valuable merchandise.

Illustration by Joaquim Alves Gaspar after a nautical chart by cartographer Jorge de Aguiar (1492).

The slave and goods trade had been developed centuries ago from all corners of the Beautiful Lands, across the Sahara to North Africa and the Mediterranean, long before the Europeans arrived.

The *Santa Maria do Cabo's* "cargo" could have been sold to the French, the Spanish or the Portuguese – whoever needed valuable, strong working hands to help explore new lands and build new settlements. Or they could have been sent deep into the tropical forests to search for gold, as suggested by some slave traders who had heard about the yellow treasure from early French corsairs and from the new natives of this side of the Atlantic, pejoratively referred to as "Indians."

Only a little over 300 black Africans survived the Atlantic crossing, and among those who perished were almost all of Abimbola's relatives. He lost his uncle to mistreatment and disease, and his cousin, who cried in despair when he saw his father's inert body being unchained so as to be tossed into the raging sea, as happened to so many others during the voyage. His cousin was a strong, healthy youth who was cast into the sea to be with his dead father; an exemplary punishment to all who could still see and hear, to those who could still feel.

The *Santa Maria do Cabo* set sail from Cape Verde in 1530. In the meantime, Martim Afonso de Souza, a Portuguese *fidalgo* and military colonial administrator, was at the Royal Palace of Sintra being commissioned by King João III of Portugal. De Souza was a personal friend of the king, as chief captain of a fleet composed of the flagship, the *nao São Miguel*, the galleon *São Vicente* and the caravels *Rosa* and *Princesa*. His mission would be to chase away the French corsairs and explorers, thus ensuring Portuguese control of the new territory of Brazil comprised by the Portuguese side of the Treaty of Tordesilhas, which had divided the territory of what Spanish and Portuguese navigators had originally thought to be part of the "West Indies," including what is known today as South America.

According to the terms of the treaty, signed in Tordesilhas in 1494, territories lying east of an imaginary meridian 370 leagues west of the Cape

Verde Islands would belong to Portugal and the lands to the west of this meridian would belong to Spain. The Tordesilhas Line, then, became the first official frontier of Brazil, establishing a long coastline which would soon play a central role in the disembarkation of slaves arriving from several different African ports, and belonging to various ethnic groups.

The success of Martim Afonso de Souza may have contributed to what would later constitute a beautiful and rich human and cultural diversity, brought to Brazil through its main ports of entry in Maranhão, Pernambuco, Bahia and Rio de Janeiro, from the sixteenth to the nineteenth century.

Abimbola and his fellow countrymen were not allowed to choose a port. In these four years of *senzala*, they had heard terrible tales about their people arriving in this new land as early as 1502. Strange languages were spoken then, and strange languages were still spoken now.

In this year of 1535, there were so many black slaves coming from Africa, of so many origins and ages, and on so many ships, that not even the Portuguese traders could identify their origins, nor were they interested in their ethnicity. This was an indifference that would contribute to the richness of a nation.

Abioye Akindele was Abimbola's twin brother. Like his older brother and every brother in the whole world, from rich castles of Europe to noble Tuareg tents made of goatskins in the deserts of Africa, he had a simple dream: He wanted to find the right girl, get married according to the Yorùbá traditions that he had seen in his homeland, and be happy. Abioye was a proud and religious young man. He would often quietly consult his favorite òrìsà, Ògún, the divinity who controls fire, the making of iron artifacts, war, craftsmanship and inventions. But he would be careful enough to ask Olúfón – the old and wise òrìsà – for help, as Ògún is also known to be unpredictable, for he has a restless spirit after having gone through too many wars and killed too many enemies.

Olabode Idowu Akindele was the youngest of the three brothers. He was 16 when he last saw Africa. To him, his family was always a panoramic experience. Of royal descent, Olabode knew he could learn many trades, explore many cultures, cross many boundaries. A dreamer from birth, he was young enough not to bear the burdens of responsibility, but old enough to learn some of the family's traditions and skills.

Like his people, Olabode was an inlander – yet he loved to eat fish from the countless rivers and lakes of his homeland. He enjoyed remembering one great adventure that his family undertook to the coast of the Gulf of Guinea, where he ate salt-water shrimp for the first time in his then 12 years of life. His father liked to call these annual voyages of explorations "a search for Olódùmarè," or "a search for ọ́rọ́ọlá." Sometimes he called it simply ọgbọ́n or àkóso, choosing the motif from one of the impressive and vastly rich collections of ancient sacred parables in the Odù Ifá, a binary system of divination from Yorùbá mythology, which, according to oral traditions, is said to contain all ancient knowledge.

Being a war hero, a diplomat, a craftsman and a trader, Olabode's father had seen some unknown sides of Africa. He had been in contact with the diverse arts, cultures, peoples and languages; ate different foods; and navigated different waters on his large dugout canoes, some of which he carved himself from oganwo and baobab woods.

Olabode's father led a troop of 80 brave and curious men and women for around 200 kilometers on their ọko through the ọsun River southwards through central Yorubaland in southwestern Nigeria, down to Lekki, through Yewa and to Eko. Sometimes, where their ọko couldn't pass, they would walk, camp, hunt, and go up and around mountains of exotic flora and fauna into what is now called the Lagos Lagoon.

Olabode and his noble family and countrymen navigated from the Sokoto down to the Niger, from beautiful Garoua to Makurdi. They crossed Nigeria and the Yorubaland and explored unknown lands. From the Niger down to what are known today as Jebba, Lakoja, Asaba, Okpai, Abo; from the Nun River down to Forcados and to the Atlantic coast, through the swamps in the Niger Delta, lakes and distributaries; from Badagry to Lagos through

Lagos Lagoon to Epe and into Lekki Lagoon, the Akindele and their men were explorers as good and as fierce as the Europeans, only they were seeking ọgbọ́n, making diplomacy in pre-colonial times, making àlàáfíà – peace – which was also rare in pre-colonial Africa.

Akindele Abimbola Olujimi made his last diplomatic exploration voyage with his family. He wanted to achieve peace and to trade with other tribes of Nigeria and Yorubaland, and with the Oyo Empire. He left Adágún Lẹ́wà, the ìlàjú founded by his ancestors in West Africa, high above Ife, where his most remote ancestors were born, above Ogbomosho and Kishi, in the beautiful, unknown wetlands of West Nigeria. They dreamt to visit Kétou, "the promised land," on their way back to Adágún Lẹ́wà.

Akindele and his wife, Titilayo, taught each of their children. Their daughters were talented in working irun orí and irungígẹ́, making art with hair, a Yorùbá tradition. These activities constituted the primary source of cultural knowledge and elevation in Yorubaland, such was the importance of the head and hair in Yorùbá society and religion, which was also used to reinforce political power.

They were good traders, known as alajapa, elepe and alaso. Abeni Adetoun Akindele was the oldest daughter, and Ololara Adeola, her sister, was the youngest of the children. They were considered princesses in Adágún Lẹ́wà. Together with their mother, and through organized guilds called egbe, which coordinated their economic activities, they learned how to trade fruits and herbs, palm oil of igi ọpẹ from their own farm and woven goods, such as aso-oke, a hand loomed cloth woven by Yorùbá men and women in pre-colonial times. These incredible women were masters of their trade. They used their looms to weave beautiful dyed cloths made of fibers from raffia palms and knew how to make fabric from the bark of fig trees – ancient and inherited knowledge, or as the Yorùbá say, ọgbọ́n. They were economically independent women in pre-colonial Africa.

These two beautiful girls had their own story to tell. They were once harassed by slave patrols near Ife on a trade caravan with their mother,

Titilayo, and some guards from Adágún Lẹ̀wà. Titilayo would always remember that she had to buy their freedom from Nkiruka Ikeotuonye, a very wealthy and powerful Igbo woman who was said to have more than 1,000 slaves on her farms.

Prince Akindele was a master carver and sculptor. However, as ọmọ ọba of Adágún Lẹ̀wà, he was in charge of the kingdom's education as well as of the family farm, which consisted mainly of a large natural territory of fruit such as fig and enset, cultivation of watermelons, vegetable crops such as Bambara groundnuts, black-eyed pea, okra and yam, ornamental and medicinal orchids, herbs such as amaranth (efo tete), used both as a vegetable and as ornamentals, and flowers for extracting various natural dyes. The family also ran an ingenious hunting operation, where hunters would keep half their game for themselves and their families while the other half would become part of the King's (and the kingdom's) own livestock – except for the delicious Ìgbín (aginiṣọ), which were collected and eaten along the journey.

These hunters had the advantage of working in a skilful team, and they were organized in such a way as to also bring home treated animal hides, furs and feathers to supply women's egbe with garments and goods for their own craftsmanship and further trade.

Prince Akindele's team of hunters was composed primarily of good warriors, trained from the ancestral need to protect the Yorùbá against enslavement by other African kingdoms – including the Yorùbá themselves. Akindele had heard from his father, who had heard from his father, that there were many slaves throughout Africa, not only in Yorubaland and Nigeria.

In most states of pre-colonial Africa, around one-third of the populations were enslaved in West Africa, from the Atlantic coast to the two banks of the Niger. Down the Niger, among the Yorùbá and the Bantu-speaking peoples, slavery had become a major business before the Portuguese and the French arrived.

Oral traditions would say that, in some states, slaves were not transferable from one master to another – they had rights and could own property and sometimes even their own slaves. Notwithstanding, the same oral traditions would remind Akindele of hundreds of years of trans-Saharan trade, which linked Western Africa to the Mediterranean world on the cultural and intellectual levels at the same time black Africans were transported to the Islamic empire across the Sahara, through Morocco and Tunisia, Chad and Libya, coming from West Africa; along the Nile from East Africa and up the coast of East Africa to the Persian Gulf – hundreds of years before the Europeans arrived.

Akindele heard these and many other stories. He knew he wouldn't go that far in his lifetime, as his father, the king, had reached either the lands of his dreams or of the stories he had heard and passed on to his son. ọmọ ọba Akindele was preparing himself to tell his own stories to his sons and daughters.

Prince Akindele and his men had traded goods and culture with the Edo people, with the Bantu, Igbos and with the Hausa people. With the Bantu, iron tips for weapons were exchanged for livestock and medicinal herbs. From their interactions with the Hausa, many of his warriors inherited the fighting techniques of Kokuwa traditional wrestling and Dambe traditional boxing; some were skilled in Hausa or Yorùbá percussive drum music; others, such as the older teenage girls, were skilled in ritualistic dances. Some men were proficient in the Yorùbá form of wrestling, or in Kadjia and Evala, their regional, but quite similar fighting forms, and a few who were from the king's and the prince's personal guards were also excellent stick fighters.

Akindele had heard tales of ancient migrations of Bantu-speaking peoples to lands further south of Yorubaland, all the way from western to eastern territories of Africa. He had heard of excellent woven textiles and jewelry from farther west, coming from the Mali Empire, which covered the first half of the Niger, and of superb metalworking and agricultural methods from various cultures in northeastern Africa.

He was curious of the new Yorùbá civilizations he heard were very powerful further to the west, in Kétou, Tado, Notsé, and along the western coastal areas.

Akindele wanted to have the great honor to explore these new cultures and civilizations in future voyages, and to share this new knowledge with his sons and daughters.

When the first Portuguese explorers arrived on the coast of Africa, they found a savanna region containing small and medium-sized kingdoms. These kingdoms were based on a combined trading system of farm products as well as an impressive commercial network, structured along the trans-Saharan routes in the west, through the Nile valley in the northeast, along the Indian Ocean routes in the east and along the Niger to the south, towards the Atlantic. All evident possible routes were explored centuries before the arrival of the European ethnocentric traditions.

These sorts of urban kingdoms had populations of 30 to 40 thousand loyal subjects, which remained within ethnically defined borders, where people of different cultures and languages lived in separate areas. Their economic and political organizations were stable, and included a strong presence of female leadership over several egbe, and a clear dedication to the education and preparation of their children for normally predefined tasks in their culturally complex society.

Among forest regions, smaller local kingdoms of a few thousand square kilometers developed in relative isolation, usually with several hundred or thousand productive inhabitants. These regions comprised the regular rain forests and the more aquatic wetlands of western Nigeria, a slightly elevated territory of beauty replete with waterfalls and fishery, and magnificent flora and fauna – where Adágún Lẹ́wà was located.

When Akindele and his family initiated their last African journey to stumble onto the *Santa Maria do Cabo* in 1530, Adágún Lẹ́wà had a population of over ten thousand and no slaves. Trade of goods amongst other kingdoms was on the rise, although distant from the decision center of the great Oyo Empire. Adágún Lẹ́wà had risen to preeminence through wealth gained from trade and its great knowledge of medicinal plants. Education was also a high priority among the people of Adágún Lẹ̀wà. Children and youth had the opportunity to learn about the adults' trade and choose their own future in the kingdom, subject to approval of a council of teachers composed mainly of prominent elder citizens.

Officials from political units made sure Adágún Lẹ̀wà stayed away from the points of convergence of the trade routes – one of the reasons the kingdom developed an advance scouting system to help trace secret and guarded routes, which would later allow for a high standard commercial flux among the Yorùbá, Hausa and Igbo peoples – and the Adja-Yorùbá descendants who migrated to the west.

In his final African journey, ọmọ ọba Akindele wanted to trade with the Edo people.

Akindele, Titilayo, Abimbola, Abioye, Olabode, Abeni and Ololara and his countrymen were ambushed by the Okpe, Edo people of Urhobo. The Edo hunters came from hidden moats strategically spread all over their land, near the village of Urhuapele, today known as Sapele, along the Benin River – through which they were rushed down to Oburuto, one of the first slave trade ports on the coast of Africa that was first reached by the Portuguese travelers some time between 1472 and 1485.

Akindele and his family were beaten and whipped, captured by organized raiding parties with traps and hunting nets made of raffia fibers, bows and arrows, clubs, wooden spears, cages – and greed. The fight was fierce but the 80 Yorùbá braves were outnumbered by the equally fierce and brave Edo men, and were taken to the *Santa Maria do Cabo* and traded for European goods and guns. Those who resisted were executed on the spot or were so badly wounded that they were not worth one miserable old copper ceitil – the coin of the lowest value in Portugal at the time. The wounded were left to die or were lucky enough to escape. Some did escape – only to be caught later and sent on the next ships to Brazil, a profitable activity which took place officially from the sixteenth to the nineteenth century.

Hundreds of people were packed side by side, chained to each other below deck on the *Santa Maria do Cabo* and taken to Cape Verde, where enslaved Africans from Senegambia and Upper Guinea, from the Adja-Yorùbá peoples of the west and from the remote Kongo-Angola regions, were waiting to join the precious cargo.

The Atlantic crossing took three tortuous months, from Cape Verde to the safe bay which, in 1501, was baptized with the name Bahia de Todos os Santos (All Saints Bay), where today lies the city of Salvador, in the state of Bahia, northeast of Brazil.

Among these African citizens of the sixteenth century were two young boys who had been separated from their families. Ololara tried to communicate with one of them, but he spoke a different language. He was soon nicknamed "Bambara" because of his many bumps on the head, which resembled the jugo beans and the nyimo beans which Titilayo used to trade back in her motherland – not without a touch of sarcasm to heal the day with some rare laughter.

Young Bambara had been almost beaten to death with wooden clubs used in his capture by his hunters from a tribe far away south of Yorubaland. As the Akindele would later discover, "Bambara" was not a very suitable name for the young boy from the Kingdom of Kongo.

The other boy, Dangbo, a strong, well-fit young man, could understand and speak Ololara's language; he told her that he came from the Kingdom of Tado and that he was experienced in metalworking and was being prepared by his father, a military chief, to be a warrior and protect his people on the next "great migration of the Adja."

While trying to survive the *Santa Maria do Cabo*, Akindele managed to remind the family that there was still something memorable and soothing to their bodies and souls: the fact that there were no slaves in Adágún Lẹ́wà. Titilayo told it a million times to her children and to her people.

Abioye Akindele, Abimbola's twin brother, liked to remember his people as a unit. No matter the origin, they were all from Africa. They were all so different from these "ugly white funny-dressed men of the big ọkọ̀." He still struggled to understand the need for war in a land of so much space and so much food. So much beauty, as he recalled on every hard day at the *feitoria* of *pau-brasil*, a large trading post of woods and exotic goods. He would talk to Olódùmarè and ask for àlàáfíà. He wished ìbáṛẹ – harmony and friendship of men and languages. No white man cared to even try to understand. These African people, no matter if noble by heritage or by heart, were the "New Orphans" of the world.

We are now in 1534. For the last three years, the Akindele managed to make as much contact as possible with other members of their *senzala*. No slave had ever escaped captivity. Many who tried were caught and tortured to death. Some were slaughtered, with the others made to watch.

The search for gold had been secretly going on since 1533 through the partnership with local natives, who received garments, tools and all kinds of gadgets in exchange for information on the best sites to get wood and find gold. As extra help, the "Indians" would also join the *capitão do mato*, a kind of foreman of the Portuguese farms in charge of capturing and punishing runaway slaves, in their search for the fugitives in the wilderness.

All the wood would go to the Portuguese crown, and all the gold to the personal chest of the *feitor*, the man in charge of the *feitorias*.

On one occasion, the Portuguese second-in-command and brother of the *feitor* was bitten by a small, beautiful snake with red, white and black colored bandings. He died hours later, to the despair of his brother, who became short of one valuable and trusted field worker, his treasurer – and gold watcher.

On a subsequent – and more dramatic – occasion, Akindele and Abimbola were cutting *pau-brasil*, with a crew of men when the *feitor* came on his usual raid. Whip in one hand, sword on his waist and followed by a troop of musketeers with their matchlocks, the Portuguese *fidalgo* wanted to show his power and keep his slaves tamed. Instead, he had Abimbola shot dead on the spot by his guard when the future king of Adágún Lẹ̀wà suddenly raised his ax towards him. What the *feitor* did not know is that Abimbola's ax was aimed at the *jararaca* snake that had come from under the leaves and was heading quickly for his leg. The irony was the second ax, which decapitated the snake a split second before it bit him. It was thrown by Akindele before he had a chance to realize his son had been murdered.

As a future king, Akindele quickly found that he could not act as a father. He knew he should act as a leader. Down on his knees, desperately crying over his son's body, he grabbed the dead headless snake in one hand and offered it to a surprised *feitor*, while holding his dead son's body with the other. A useless, starving, common and nearly naked black slave in his rags had just saved the life of the dressed-up, armored *feitor*. A ragged but wise nobleman dressed in his honor wanted to save a nation.

Akindele understood the words *"Obrigado, negro."* That was perhaps the first time a high-ranked slave-owner had ever spoken to a black slave in this new-found land of Brazil. That night Pero Castelo Coelho, the *feitor*, had Akindele sent to his quarters at the *casa grande* – the "big house," as it was called – the headquarters of the *feitoria*. The *feitor* also had a family in Portugal and wanted to bring his wife and children to the new land. He had slaves enough to build a new and larger home at the *feitoria*, and the Crown was satisfied with his work – but not as much as he himself was with his own gold.

That night Akindele saw hope as the *feitor* needed more trustworthy men to help organize and control the next "bulk of slaves" coming from Africa, as gold was abundant and a new kind of wood called *jacarandá* had been discovered and had become highly valued. A kind of rosewood, which produced a very good and resistant timber, the *jacarandá* was soon used for building floors, furniture, platters and kitchen utensils that would later be spread throughout the rich properties of the colony.

Pero Castelo Coelho tried to communicate with Akindele, using a passage of the Bible where St. Paul recommends "the good servant to serve well his Christian owner." He also offered Akindele clean clothes – and the position of "slave watcher" at the *feitoria*.

Akindele had seen and tasted many fruits in his four years in Bahia. With his sparse Portuguese and the help of some poor translating, he felt he could bargain with the *feitor* for better food for his people, promising that, if well fed and better treated, they would produce more in turn and that he could arrange "to amuse the bosses with demonstrations of music, dance and acrobatic skills from Africa to please the *feitor* any time he wished." Akindele also offered to build fish traps on the seashore in order to increase fishing productivity with less effort. If production increased, the slaves would be allowed to eat part of the surplus, hence being more productive and thankful "to their masters and bosses."

These fish traps were artificial pools consisting of low stone walls built of natural beach cobbles and local rocks. These ingenious traps would allow all kinds of fish to enter the pools during high tide and trap them during low tide, when men could collect them effortlessly.

As the *feitor* became increasingly interested, Akindele added that some of the men could even build boats and make fishnets out of raffia strings, to catch fresh water fish in the surrounding rivers. Once laid in the water, these nets could be hauled into the boats with the fish. Akindele assured the *feitor* that he could identify which slaves had all these specific skills to help the development and economic growth of the *feitoria*. Prince Akindele Abimbola Olujimi knew about diplomacy, leadership, teaching, and about a profitable and organized production. His family had been doing it in Adágún Lẹ̀wà for many years.

The meeting went on for hours, the conversation recorded by the official scribe of the *feitoria*. An agreement was struck, most probably the first "contract" ever made between an African slave and his master in the new territories.

Fish, shrimp and raw oysters were added to the slaves' diet, as well as chicken, which had been taken to Portugal from Tamil Nadu, south of India, by Portuguese navigators and brought to Brazil in the early colonial years. However, heavy chains and handcuffs still awaited the disobedient and the lazy slave at the *senzala*.

As grieving was not allowed, Abimbola was to be remembered only when fortune brought them peace. However, the rest of Akindele's family was safer. Titilayo became head of the maids in the *casa grande*, helping the wives and daughters of the Europeans with cooking tasks. Abeni and Ololara were maids and "special servants" of the *capitão do mato*. Ololara was the favorite concubine of the *feitor*, and stayed most of the time at the *casa grande* helping her mother with domestic duties.

Titilayo was worried. She had heard about an Igbo woman who had all her teeth taken by the wife of the *capitão do mato* because she had a beautiful smile, whereas the Portuguese woman had lost a front tooth during a storm on her journey to Brazil, which had left her feeling ugly. And she was right! But now that the beautiful Igbo black woman was toothless, the *capitão do mato* no longer wanted her. He wanted Abeni. And he had her, always out of his wife's sight. He had to be extra careful with Princess Ololara, though – the most beautiful daughter – or the *feitor* could have his eyes gouged out.

With the death of Abimbola, Prince Abioye's father appointed him responsible for the future of the young generation and of all who supported the secret development of a plan to escape to the wilderness with as many people as possible.

Olabode had made friends with Bambara. Both young men had been exchanging cultural and language information. With the agreement between Akindele and the *feitor*, more people were able to join the little melting pot of their *senzalas*. Akindele made this possible by convincing most slaves to work hard, refrain from complaining, hide sickness whenever possible and obey their masters blindly, all in exchange for better food and greater trust.

Those who did not comply were tortured. Many did not survive illness and maltreatment. Others, who for ethnic reasons did not accept Akindele's leadership, were left on their own. They too organized groups of escapees. Most died trying. Many even preferred to die as their own demonstration of punishment to the *feitor*. They knew that having fewer slaves would reduce the *feitoria's* profit. So they simply killed themselves by trying to escape carelessly, or by drowning themselves in the rivers or at sea.

By the end of 1534 the 300 slaves who had survived the journey on the *Santa Maria do Cabo* were down to 180.

The Feitoria Real da Bahia was a large settlement – and one of the first of Ilha de Vera Cruz – established in 1502 in Bahia by one of the young noble crew members brought by explorer Gaspar de Lemos in his expedition to the new land in 1501. Several times the *feitoria* was attacked by the local natives and destroyed. Many Portuguese lives were taken. It was rebuilt by the now not-so-young and not-so-noble, but still brave Portuguese, of whom there is no historical record, with the help of expeditionary Fernão de Magalhães in 1514. It was attacked by the French and rebuilt in 1529 by Pero Castelo Coelho, who first ordered the 400 African black slaves be brought by the captain of the *Santa Maria do Cabo* and made friends with the "Indians."

The large *feitoria* had some 20 houses, one being a small fortress for the military troops, a small chapel, a makeshift hospital and a tall tower made of stone, used by military sentinels.

With Akindele's arrival in 1531, the Feitoria Real da Bahia had four *senzalas*, each with 100 slaves who would be trapped in such dwellings from 8 pm to 4 am every day except on Sundays. The *feitor* knew that slaves were valuable merchandise, so they would have to eat and rest "once in a while, like humans do." So they ate mangos and oranges, which were planted along trade routes by the first European explorers in order to prevent scurvy. Their diet consisted mainly of manioc flour mixed with water. Occasionally, the "best slaves" would "deserve" some fresh meat, although the *uru*, a native kind of wild partridge, was also widely – and generally secretly – consumed.

Akindele's efforts were well rewarded. By 1534 most of the 180 slaves who remained from the original group of the *Santa Maria do Cabo* were now eating local fruits such as guava, passion fruit, cashew, araçá and tarumã, which they gathered during their incursions into the wilderness to cut timber or find gold. His strategically selected group of "artists" had special permission to return to the *senzala* at 6 o'clock to rehearse the demonstration for the upcoming party prepared by the *feitor*. His impressive fishing methods and craftsmanship also worked, and soon he had to organize a team of woodcarvers to build canoes, which were then traded for more information on gold sites and for convenient maintenance of friendship with the local "Indians."

From his newly formed team of artists, Akindele extracted their best skills. From Titilayo, Ololara and Abeni, conveniently chosen to be part of the group, would come the beautiful hair of the artists; the Adja would put up a show of back flips and front flips, while the Hausa and Yorùbá were in charge of playing the drums, which were made with the help of Abioye and his father, with *jacarandá* and *acaju* wood, deer and ocelot skin, and raffia, while the few Bantu speaking people built several single-string musical instruments resembling a bow, made of *biriba* wood – the *ombumbumba,* as it was called by some of the slaves. It had a gourd resonator attached to the back of the string bearer.

Everyone rehearsed to the music for the *feitor's* party. Secretly, in the *senzala*, though, they practiced and taught each other techniques of stick-fighting, wrestling and boxing, while the girls rehearsed the *efundula* dance.

In the beginning, a total of 80 people formed the "team of artists," among them slaves from several distinct regions of West Africa and Kongo-Angola, forming one of the greatest social mixes of slaves in human history.

The first official presentation of African arts and culture at the *feitoria* took place on September 29, 1534, the *feitor's* birthday.

To an amused *feitor*, wondering why so many slaves took part in the show, Akindele tried to explain that in Africa, according to tradition, music is transmitted orally and, in a typical performance, a chorus of singers must echo a soloist around a circle of participants, so that the music is "trapped" and therefore contagious to both participants and spectators.

To an amused Akindele, Bambara, a son of the Bantu migrations to the Kongo State, and Dangbo, the young warrior from the Adja kingdom of Tado, and a direct descendant of the Yorùbá, had the best performances among all the artists and their talent should be recognized and rewarded. The two young men, now inseparable friends, were indeed rewarded with the responsibility to help Abioye lead a group of self-sufficient people, who would be able to explore faraway inland territory and establish a hidden community to prosper independently and free, if Akindele's plans worked.

Akindele and Titilayo knew they wouldn't be able to make it. When the time came, they should distract their masters with good work and good cooking and housekeeping. Most of all, they should be trustable servants for at least one more year, when a new ship would come bringing more slaves from Africa – and more responsibility to Akindele. His plan was to be the most reliable servant in the *feitoria* and make sure his group of artists got bigger and practiced for the next party, when the wife of the *feitor* would arrive with their children to be with him in the now rich *feitoria*.

After the new shipment of slaves arrived, Akindele became very unpopular, an extra burden for the man once destined to be a king.

From one of the Yorùbá newcomers, a loyal subject, he heard that Adágún Lẹ́wà had been attacked by the Oyo Empire with a cavalry of thousands of men and that most of the Yorùbá slaves on board the ship were former prisoners of war, who were enslaved in order to ensure total dominance by the Oyo Empire. In 1535 the peaceful kingdom of Adágún Lẹ́ wà no longer existed. It became a trading post and a strategic warehouse for the Oyo Empire in their quest for additional power. The king and his closest collaborators were killed. Thousands of free citizens were made slaves. Most were sold to European slave traders. At last, Akindele was the king.

From the captain of the slave ship, the *feitor* heard that King Dom João III of Portugal, planning to initiate a project of systematic colonization of Brazil, had divided the territory into 15 strips of land that ran along the coast, and from the coast up to the border of the Tordesilhas line. These strips of land, called *capitanias hereditárias* (heritable captaincies), were given to 12 Portuguese noblemen, ranked *capitão-mor* (the captain-major, the local military highest authority) or *donatários* (donataries, the grantees), who were vested with extraordinary powers over their vast new and unknown domains. Some profitable *feitorias*, such as the Feitoria Real da Bahia, still retained their status. But the *feitor* was not happy for not being among the 12 chosen new "lords of the lands."

Pero Castelo Coelho knew that more control would eventually come from Portugal, and he became worried about his secret gold operations. The *feitor* needed more men at work, more wood, and of course more gold. Therefore, he had to count on all the help he could from his men and from his "best slaves" in order to make the newcomers work hard. So he asked Akindele to rehearse with more men for an even bigger party he was now planning to put on for the new Donatário of the Capitania da Bahia de Todos os Santos, which comprised his *feitoria*, as well as to celebrate the arrival of his wife and daughters. The *feitor* set a date: September 29 of the year 1536.

King Akindele knew he would have his best chance in the last five years of irons and irony. Despite the agreement with the *feitor*, native African citizens continued to be brutalized, branded with hot irons and chained to one another at the *feitoria* until Akindele could guarantee that they were tamed and loyal, which was rather difficult due to the differences among them in language, culture and ideals, especially among the newcomers. So he worked hard and tried to make his men work as hard as possible. By 1536 nearly 500 slaves were working at the Feitoria Real da Bahia. The "group of artists" grew to become a team of 200 strong, well-trained and intelligent African natives of various ethnic origins, all well fed and ready for action.

For the next several months, the Portuguese masters could hear the sounds of music and dance and the clapping of hands, as the performers rehearsed for the forthcoming party. A new group of young men brought from the highlands of Benguela, a province of Angola, helped Akindele put on a show of the *efundula,* using the male's vigorous prelude dance in a theatrical competition between warriors for the hand of a young bride; then, the "brides-to-be" would dance their beautiful, sensual dance. Akindele saw the practice of African fighting arts and body abilities as indispensable to his escape plan, and he knew that loyalty, music and culture, along with the sound of timber being piled and of gold being poured into the hidden chests of the *casa grande*, should conceal any suspicion. By September 1536 his original group of artists would have been practicing (and eating and sleeping better) for almost two years.

On September 29, 1536, on a night lit by a big fire and hundreds of whale oil lamps, the *feitor*, his family, his guests – Francisco Pereira Coutinho, the first Donatário of Bahia de Todos os Santos, their scribes, Portuguese contractors, naval officers and noblemen, captains of the woods, military personnel, physicians, their families and Catholic priests from the two headquarters – were about to watch a spectacular demonstration of ingenious African minds not to be forgotten for generations.

Akindele had divided the presentation into five parts. In the first part, ten drums were played in dramatic rhythm, announcing a group of "stick dancers." Young Dangbo led twenty stick fighters disguised as dancers to perform athletic and acrobatic moves and to show keen control of their wooden sticks. The men were careful enough not to make too great a show of fighting skills, and thereby warn their masters.

The frenetic rhythm of the drums continued loudly, as the twenty men left the stage to make room for the next group of 20 beautiful, naked young female *efundula* dancers.

Ten men joined the drummers and started playing their *ombumbumbas* before the group of dancers came onstage. Singing and clapping began. At this point, Akindele surprised the crowd with a superb demonstration of servility. He called a group of forty slaves who were not part of his original team of artists. The men came onstage, chained to one another in twos, which brought a sense of tranquility to a perplexed *feitor*. The men in their shackles quickly offered the guests a taste of port wine and a new original thick and sweet drink made with fresh water and mango. It was a surprise to the *feitor* with the blessing of a stoned *capitão do mato*.

Titilayo too had done her work very well. For almost two years she had learned to prepare poisonous drinks and food with a mixture of Atlantic forest vines used by the native "Indians" to fish, paralyze and kill their pray. The effects had been carefully tested by Akindele while fishing and hunting and during the preparation of meals at the *casa grande* on the monkeys and wild dogs that always appeared near the kitchen begging for food. Dizziness, dysentery and death were a constant result. Intoxication and dazedness were her best result. Titilayo had silently contributed her share of participation to the success of Akindele's "group of artists." It was the share of a real queen. Had she been caught, she would have been killed with her entire family and the plan would have been aborted indefinitely.

When the next group of women dancers entered the stage, the second group, the "stick dancers," had already killed a dozen Portuguese guards on their way out of the *feitoria* with their sharp and resilient sticks made of biriba wood, a flexible and yet highly resistant wood that seldom breaks when used as whips, clubs, or spears.

Most of the Portuguese men were completely astonished by such beauty, divided between the exotic and the erotic, drunk with joy and, at the same time, confused, with a mixture of gloom and euphoria, seeing more colors than there were to be seen and hearing more noise then there was to be heard. Most of the women tried to hold onto their husbands, intimately outraged on one hand and socially desolated on another, displaced in their prerogatives, yet challenged in their spirit.

The fourth group finished its presentation in impressive style, with the naked female slaves running around the *feitoria* with a small and inoffensive lit torch, so as to "invoke the goddess of light" as Akindele explained to the *feitor*, "to bless those of the *feitoria* and the *capitania* with the fire of life."

The fifth group never made it to the stage. The forty servants bearing wine and juice went to each of the houses of the *feitoria* to offer the drinks to those who were on guard and, therefore, could not attend the party. To them, the servants offered the same wines and juices and to the houses, mostly made of wood, they secretly served a dose of whale oil "to bless their doors."

In the riot, the houses which had been "blessed by the whale oil" were promptly set on fire by the group of naked dancers on their way out of the *feitoria*, protected by the fifth group of artists, of Dangbo's Adja fighters.

As the whole *feitoria* caught on fire, the warriors of the fifth group gave their tools and axes to the leaders of the other *senzalas*, where at least 350 slaves were locked in chains. The forty poor souls chained in twos were the first to be massacred, and only a few survived.

On September 29 of the year 1536 more than 300 slaves managed to escape the Feitoria Real da Bahia and were never caught. Among them were Bambara, Dangbo, Abioye, Olabode and three-months pregnant Ololara.

Akindele, Titilayo and Abeni are said to have returned to Africa on a French ship. Many slaves escaped their shackles during the "war of the Feitoria." Pero Castelo Coelho fell in disgrace with the *donatário* and with King Dom João III, and the Feitoria Real da Bahia was finally burned down by the "Indians." No one ever heard about it.

Dangbo became the military leader of the group, the very first organized settlement of runaway slaves in Brazilian territory, which Bambara and his people named Mukambu, with Abioye Akindele as the new king.

Oral traditions say that Bambara and Ololara had performed the *efundula* ceremony somewhere in the beautiful inlands of Brazil in 1537.

It is possible that, in 1537, inspired by mythological Odùduwà, from whom, according to oral history, all Yorùbá kings descended, the Akindele still kept their Africa alive.

The Akindele story could have been even richer than the one told on these pages, for the early trans-Saharan routes, followed by all other African slave routes, were also used to exchange men and women with ideas, rather than just labor and goods.

The first 12 ships that arrived in Brazil with explorer Pedro Álvares Cabral in the 1500s were the precursors of the thousands of Portuguese caravels and slave ships that officially engaged in the Atlantic slave trade between Africa and Brazil, every year, until the nineteenth century. When the American schooner *Mary E. Smith* arrived bringing the last cargo of slaves – 400 free people she tried to smuggle into Brazilian territory – almost half died. It was the last time we heard of a slave ship in Brazil.

This story could have happened with many of the more than five million African citizens brought from their homelands to Brazil in almost four centuries of slave trade.

# LORDS OF THE ATLANTIC

I n order to better understand the age of Exploration and the great navigations that fostered the Atlantic slave trade – which culminated in the development of capoeira in Brazil, and in a number of rich Afro-cultural expressions elsewhere in the Americas – we shall travel back to the year 1415, when the Master of the Order of Aviz, King John I of Portugal and the Algarve, conquered the city of Celta on the North African side of the Strait of Gibraltar from the king of Morocco. King John was influenced by his third child, Prince Henry the Navigator, who was fascinated with the scientific approach of the maritime navigations, and with what he thought were endless possibilities of expansion of the Portuguese trade in Africa.

More than military achievements, the first European conquests of Africa would not only later become an age of discoveries and the establishment of the "New World," but it would also influence populations and cultures, and

Illustration by Bruno Tavares based on the work of Brian Boru, Cross-Order the Aviz (2006).

the formation of a cradle of peoples and geopolitical changes that would reshape the modern world.

After the successful venture in Celta, the Portuguese, now under the leadership of King Eduard, Henry's eldest brother, continued encouraging Portugal's maritime explorations of Africa, with Henry's support and incentive. When Eduard died and his son Afonso V came of age after ten years of regency, the young king – the 12th King of Portugal and the Algarves – continued aiming at expanding Portugal's maritime conquests.

# The Portuguese Slave Trade

The first cargo of slaves from Africa was not taken to Brazil, or to any conquered land in the New World, but to the islands of Azores, Santa Maria and São Miguel, between 1427, when Diogo da Silva first explored the islands for the Portuguese, and 1432. The cargo was taken by Gonçalo Velho, considered to be the first Portuguese settler of the area. Between 1433 and 1434, Portuguese navigator and explorer Gil Eanes had sailed from Lagos, in the Algarve, to reach the Canary Islands and was the first to sail beyond the feared Cape Bojador, for nearly 200 miles, and return.[1] The doors to West Africa and the triangular trade were beginning to open.

Later, in 1441, slaves were sold in Portugal itself, taken by Antão Gonçalves in the expedition under the command of explorer Nuno Tristão, who was the first European to land in the region of Guinea, sponsored by Prince Henry the Navigator.

The first large cargo of slaves (close to 200 of different ethnic groups) is reported to have arrived in Lagos in 1444, brought by the Portuguese explorer Laçarote de Freitas, according to royal chronicler Gomes Eanes de Azurara, whose records of the voyage were completed in 1453 but not published until 1841. The island of Arguim, off the coast of Mauritania, was discovered in the early 1440s' by the Portuguese, and was settled in 1445 by Prince Henry the Navigator, who then established the first European trading post of slaves and goods with African peoples.

In 1452 the first African slaves arrived on Madeira Island, one of the Portuguese routes to and from West Africa. By 1455 hundreds of slaves were sent to Lagos every year; from the slave market of Arguim to the infamous slave auctions of Lagos, African slaves were later supplied as merchandise to Spain and Italy and were sold in the city markets of Lisbon. The "house of slaves" is still there. I visited the place in 2001, and there was an open art exposition being held inside the house. Lagos is located near the beautiful cities of Portimão and Carvoeiro, and is around 33 km from Sagres.

The Portuguese were also the first Europeans to arrive in the Senegambia region in 1455. Venetian explorer and merchant Alvise Cadamosto, at the service of the Portuguese Crown, traded along the coast of Senegambia in this year and was also the first European to reach the Cape Verde Islands, in his 1456 voyage, after which he returned to the African coast to sail down to present-day Guinea Bissau.

Under the command of King D. Afonso V, the Portuguese navigators went on to explore North Africa and conquer Alcácer-Ceguer (al-Qsar as-Seghir) in 1458.

The first exploration of Sierra Leone and Liberia is attributed to Pedro de Sintra, between 1460 and 1462; in 1471 they conquered the strategic cities of Tangiers and Arzila.

Incomplete historical records indicate that João de Santarém and Pero Escobar were the first Europeans to discover the Gold Coast, including the islands of São Tomé and Príncipe all the way to the coast of Gabon, between 1471 and 1475.

## Pre-Colonial Accounts of Africans Enslaving Africans

Eustache de la Fosse was a Flemish explorer and merchant (and a smuggler according to the Portuguese navigators who wanted to control all the western coast of Africa), who traveled with a Spanish fleet, in 1479–1480, reaching as far as from present-day Guinea Bissau to the coast of Ghana (São Jorge da Mina). He wrote one of the first impressive records of the internal African slave trade in the Gold Coast, as he witnessed slaves being bought by Spanish traders on the Windward Coast to later "resell" them on the Gold Coast to native African traders.[2] De la Fosse reportedly witnessed two Portuguese merchant ships returning from the Bight of Biafra with a cargo of around 400 slaves to be resold on the Gold Coast. Eustache de la Fosse was captured for being in "illicit trading in Portuguese waters" by the Portuguese Captain Diogo Cão.

Diogo Cão is cited as the first European to discover, in 1482, the mouth of the River Congo, which flows through the present-day Democratic Republic of the Congo, the People's Republic of the Congo, the Central African Republic, and partially through Zambia, Angola, Cameroon, and Tanzania. Two years later the explorer reached Walvis Bay, in present-day Namibia.

We are now at the dawn of Prince Henry the Navigator's Atlantic Ocean explorations and of the Atlantic slave trade.

Afonso V, nicknamed "the African," was eventually succeeded by his son, John II, in 1481. Under King John's reign, in 1482 the Portuguese founded the fortress São Jorge da Mina (Saint George of the Mine), or simply Feitoria da Mina, which would be an important Portuguese slave trade post during the Atlantic slave trade, and which would later often suggest the name "Mina" as an ethnic group, a label some authors refer to the slaves who came from that region to Brazil. The castle of St. George of the Mine (Elmina Castle) was built on the Gold Coast, part of the Gulf of Guinea, in West Africa, in present-day Elmina, Ghana, and it is the first known European building still in existence in the region.

When the Portuguese arrived on the coastal region of Guinea, they found that the natives of the region were from the Akan linguistic group and several states were established along the coastal areas and in the inlands. The

Asante of the inlands and the Fante of the coast would soon be key players in the Atlantic slave trade.

The Fante people are part of the large Akan linguistic group of West Africa, and their early economics dealt primarily with the trade of gold and enslaved peoples with Mande and Hausa traders within Africa before the Europeans arrived. They were also related to the Adja-Yorùbá peoples who had migrated from Nigeria to Kétou and to the regions comprising present-day Benin, Togo and Ghana.

The Fante were among the first West African natives to have trade relations with the Portuguese. As a result of this direct association, members of this Akan group gradually absorbed aspects of Portuguese European culture; evidence in a number of parishes in Portugal still show the converse was also true in Portuguese society, and later in its culture and its colonies.

However, one must be naive to believe that these natives of Africa accepted slavery readily. Ultimately, the slave business led to warfare and revolts on African soil. Pockets of resistance were everywhere and were tamed with the use of extreme violence. These rebellions continued during the Atlantic slave trade both on African soil and in the Americas, where new laws were created and often revised to reduce the African resistance. The birth of the *mocambo* and *quilombo* took place much before the history of Palmares in Brazil.

## *West Africa Conquered*

In 1488 Bartolomeu Dias was the first European to round the Cape of Good Hope, present-day South Africa, and enter the Indian Ocean.

The trade of slaves with other European countries and the treaties with African nations, where the Portuguese would trade goods for African slaves captured by their own or neighboring African tribes, brought to the Portuguese Crown what was considered a new economic system, and what would later lead to a new economic era created in the New World. Nevertheless, this new economic activity triggered both prosperity and misery on the two sides of the Mediterranean. However, it would also trigger an unprecedented array of cultural richness and diversity – and later foster the unique condition that allowed the development of capoeira only in Brazil, despite the apparent similar cultural ingredients and African seeds spread all over the colonial Americas and especially in the Caribbean islands.

In Lisbon, African slaves mixed and integrated into Portuguese society. On the Azores islands, one of the Portuguese Atlantic routes, the first settlers were a mixed group of people from the Portuguese provinces of Algarve and Minho, followed by black slaves, people from Madeira Island, Moorish prisoners, French, Italians, Scots, English, and Flemings. There were petty criminals, Spanish clergy, Jews, soldiers, government officials, European merchants and sugarcane growers.[3]

Almost one hundred years of slavery and slave trade before coming to Brazil gave the Portuguese explorers the experience they would bring to the Atlantic slave trade and to their new Brazilian rural and urban settings. There, African slaves and their descendants would later engage in a variety of occupations, first in the rural activities in the *feitorias* and *engenhos* and subsequently in urban employment, mostly in domestic services.

As argued earlier, the Portuguese were influenced to a certain degree by their relations with Africa and the African peoples, a fact that cannot be denied and which can still be seen in the several parishes they named after the "Negroes," in Lisbon and all around Portugal.

Not only did the Portuguese have great cultural impact in their African colonies, but the opposite, although to a lesser degree also happened. African culture, goods and gastronomy were also being integrated into Portuguese society much before Cabral arrived on the Brazilian beaches. This African influence on European society went on from the initial colonial periods to the modern day, and were reflected all over Europe on a smaller scale, expressed in the arts, religion and culture spread throughout the world in museums and private collections.

Some people still tend to believe that the Portuguese started the Atlantic slave trade by introducing West African slaves to Brazil in the sixteenth century, but, as we have seen earlier, the mercantilism between Portugal and West Africa, sponsored by King John, was already a reality in the fifteenth century, with all its cultural and social ingredients which would later be replicated in the sixteenth-century New World and Brazilian experience.

King John sponsored the association of the Portuguese traders with West African guilds, establishing some important precedents for the Atlantic slave trade and the future colonization of Brazil, such as the *feitorias* (the "factories" – fortresses with commercial establishments). The first one, Feitoria de Fernando de Noronha, was financed by a consortium of Jewish merchants (New Christians) and led by Fernão de Loronha (a.k.a. Fernando de Noronha or Fernão de Noronha) in 1502, under contract by the Portuguese Crown, and later the *capitanias de cana de açúcar* (the sugarcane mills).

Still in 1480, the Portuguese king had sold the right to trade slaves, spices and ivory from Guinea to Bartolomeo Marchionni, a wealthy Florentine banker and merchant in Lisbon.[4] Marchionni would later be one of the financers of the expedition of Pedro Alvares de Cabral, who is regarded as the official discoverer of Brazil in 1500.

The hypothesis at stake here is the evidence of a clear connection of historical events which places similar economic interests and players in similar rural, urban and cultural settings in Europe and on the islands off the coast of Africa to those that would exist in the New World a few decades later – and in a much larger scale. These historical precedents would not only set the initial standards for the dramatically different levels of socialization of the black native of Africa in enslaved Brazil, but would also trigger the slave revolts, which started to be forged during the very first voyages of explorations to Africa in the fifteenth century. From motherland Africa to Portugal, and then to the New World, African slaves began their saga much sooner than the appearance of the Brazilian *mocambos* and *quilombos* in this historical scenario.

The Portuguese roots of the Afro-Brazilian culture are strongly present not only in the religious aspects but also in the practical aspects of the Afro-Portuguese and Afro-Brazilian societies. In an important study published in 1999, historian Linda M. Heywood calls our attention to the invaluable insights into the "transcultural process that took place in Brazil from the sixteenth to the early nineteenth century,"[5] due to the nature of the Portuguese relations with the Kingdom of Kongo and Angola between the sixteenth and eighteenth centuries. When she says that "the roots of Afro-Brazilian culture lay deep in the history of Afro-Portuguese relations,"[6] referring to the importance of the Catholic Church in the articulation of both elite and popular culture in Portugal, she is also opening a door to the evidence of a much broader concept of culture, considering that the Afro-Portuguese and Afro-Brazilian cultures are strongly attached to African original religious aspects, which have been producing a rich cultural and social environment since pre-colonial times.

Therefore, the seeds of liberty have traveled along with the slaves to the New World from the sixteenth century much as their religion and craftsmanship have followed them. The same way black slaves were used in a variety of jobs as early as in the fifteenth century on the islands of Madeira and Azores, and in Europe, sometimes employed as domestic servants, farmers and artisans, women were often put in a privileged position in the household, and some of the loyal men rose in status to become part of the crew of some Portuguese ships.

From the mid-fifteenth century to the official beginning of the Atlantic slave trade, "experienced" slaves from Madeira, Azores, the Canary Islands, Cape Verde and São Tomé, as well as the descendants from the very first who helped settle the islands, were eventually sent to Brazil and to the West Indies to work on the plantations. Alvise Cadamosto, the Venetian navigator hired by Prince Henry, wrote in 1454–1456 that each of the Portuguese ships had African native interpreters on board, brought from Portugal.

These first "socialized" slaves contributed to the formation of the very first "blend" of cultures in the enslaved New World, which represented a small but relevant bridge between the unknown and survival. For its part, Portugal also had previous experience with the sugarcane plantations and African slavery in the Algarve region and, before the African Atlantic explorations, slaves could be seen doing domestic chores, and in the courts of Italy, Spain and England.

## The Spanish Slave Trade

In 1492, after landing for the first time on the island he named San Salvador, in what is now the Bahamas, and two weeks later in Cuba, on December 5 Christopher Columbus reached the island now known as Haiti and named it Hispaniola, having Cuba to the West and Puerto Rico to the East. Hispaniola would soon become the base for further expansion of the Spanish Americas.

Columbus founded what would be the first European settlement in the New World in December of 1492 and named it La Navidad ("Christmas"). Several months later, the settlement was destroyed and its inhabitants killed by the Taíno, a subgroup of the Arawak peoples who also inhabited Cuba, Jamaica, Puerto Rico, the Bahamas and South America. There are some controversies over whether Columbus's men were killed by the Taínos due to their greedy search for gold and Taíno women, or by rival tribes.

On his second voyage, in September of 1493, Columbus founded a second settlement which he named La Isabella, in the present-day province of Puerto Plata (Port of Silver), Dominican Republic, which became the first permanent European settlement in the New World.

Columbus himself may have taken the first black slaves to the new territory. The first African slaves were taken to the island of Hispaniola in the late 1490s, or early 1500s, to help with the construction of the new settlements on the island, and later to work in the gold mines, replacing the

Taínos, who were being decimated by disease introduced by the Europeans, as a result of forced labor, or killed in rebellions against the Spanish. These slaves, known as *ladinos* or *ladinos negros* ("those who were 'Latinized' – who could speak Spanish;" by extension, "those who were smart, cunning, sly") were not originally from Africa, but born in Spain, from where they were brought and where some were born free. Those were the first African slaves brought to America.

## Ladinos and Bozales

Spain also had an early direct experience with the slave trade from Africa and the Atlantic islands. In 1476, Carlos de Valera sailed from the Bay of Biscay, in Spain, to the coast of Guinea on a mission for the Kings of Castile, and brought back to Spain a cargo of 400 African slaves.[7]

In 1503, Spain started to take Spanish-born slaves to work on the plantations of Hispaniola. As of 1505, under the rule of Nicolás de Ovando, the governor of Hispaniola appointed directly by the Catholic monarchs Ferdnand II of Aragon and Isabella de Castile – the founders of Christopher Columbus's expedition to discover the New World – hundreds of slaves were officially and systematically sent to the island together with an unknown number of smuggled slaves from Africa, known as *bozales* ("those who were not tamed," and, by extension, "those who did not speak the language, ignorant").

In 1518 merchant Lorens de Gominot was granted the first Spanish *assiento* to import 4,000 slaves directly from Africa to the Spanish Americas between that year and 1526, bringing 2,000 to Hispaniola. The *assiento* was a trade agreement through which the selected licensed traders received the monopoly over the trade of slaves between Africa and the Americas. The task was sublet to Portuguese merchant ships, since the Treaty of Tordesillas forbade the Spaniards to conduct their own African slaving expeditions.[8]

Spaniards began importing black slaves directly from Africa in order to supply the Spanish Americas with labor for the growing sugarcane plantations, the first in the New World. For a long period of time, they would maintain the hegemony of the Atlantic slave trade in the northern part of the Atlantic, while the Portuguese dominated the south Atlantic routes.

Slaves in Hispaniola now had different cultural and ethnic identities, as they came from Spain, as African descendants, as well as directly from different regions of Africa, which is one factor responsible for the establishment of the first "African melting pot" of Spanish origin (the second being the Portuguese).

## Palenques and Cumbes: The Cousins of Quilombos

Black slaves escaped from their Portuguese and Spanish masters starting in the early stages of the Atlantic slave trade. At first, they banded together for companionship and mutual support, forming organized refugee communities whose first priority was to escape from the white domination. These earlier communities varied in size and were sometimes very small, having as few as half a dozen slaves, as opposed to the general notion that "thousands of slaves lived in the *quilombos, palenques* and *cumbes,*" which later, however, would become true. In Brazil, these settlements became known by their African names as *mocambos* and *quilombos* (from *kilombu* and mukambu), and the runaway slaves were later called *Quilombolas*.

In the Spanish Hispaniola, runaway "Maroon" slaves, called *cimarrones,* escaped to the mountains and the backcountry, where they assembled with the Taíno to form the small settlements known by the Spanish as *palenques*, or *cumbes*. Some of these settlements grew to become fairly well-organized communities, not only in Hispaniola, but elsewhere in the Spanish Americas.

Here, we have an important point if we want to later understand the history of capoeira. Slaves were coming from Africa brought by Portuguese merchants from the same African sources that supplied the coast of Brazil. To illustrate an example, in 1532 the Portuguese slave ship *Santo Antônio* transported 201 slaves from the island of São Tomé, in the Gulf of Guinea, to Puerto Rico and Santo Domingo. In 1582, the Santo Antônio transported 166 slaves from West Central Africa and Luanda to Bahia, and four years later 145 slaves were shipped from the same region to Santo Domingo. The same flag, the same ships, the same regions and the same peoples did not produce the very same cultural outcome.

As seen earlier, Portugal dominated the slave trade in the sixteenth century. Spain would bring slaves to the Americas based on the trade agreement called *assiento*. The *assientos* were primarily granted to the Portuguese merchants, and African slaves began to arrive from West Africa to the Spanish Americas, initially from Guinea and Sierra Leone and later from the Kongo-Angola region. During the early seventeenth century most of the slaves were shipped to the Spanish ports from the Portuguese colony in Angola. Later in the eighteenth century, the Atlantic slave trade would be dominated by Britain and Holland, and the slaves continued to be sent mostly to the colonies in the New World.

From the sixteenth to the nineteenth century, African slaves were taken all the way from Senegambia to West Central Africa and to the kingdoms of Loango, Kongo and Ndongo. Roughly 1.6 million African slaves were taken to the Spanish Americas during the Atlantic slave trade, and over five million were taken by the British, French, Dutch and Danish slave traders during this period.

In 1697, following the Treaty of Ryswick, Spain finally conceded the western third of the original island of Hispaniola (present-day Haiti) to the French.

In 1713, the Spanish granted the last and most important *assiento* to the British, by one of the provisions in the Tratado de Paz of Utrecht, the Treaty of Utrecht, which was translated into English and printed in London in 1714 as the Treaty of Peace and Friendship. This contract entitled the South Sea Company to send 4,800 slaves to the Spanish Americas, annually, for the next 30 years.

## Adja-Yorùbá Traditions in Spanish Americas

Bantu slaves from the Kongo-Angola region accounted for over one-third of all ethnic groups imported to the Spanish island; however, they did not represent an "overwhelming majority," as some authors believe, let alone a cultural one.

## Santeria: The Cousin of the Brazilian Candomblé

Cuba also received a great part of its slave population from Dahomey (Bight of Benin). Most of these slaves were Adja-Fon, Adja-Ewe and Yorùbá (all Yorùbá related). These Adja, Fon, Ewe and Yorùbá peoples are often considered as distinct ethnic groups in a number of authors' statistics, whereas the Yorùbá were the origin of a series of migrations that gave birth to the Adja-Ewe and the Adja-Fon peoples. From Calabar, in Nigeria, the "Calibari" slaves who were imported to Cuba also shared many religious characteristics with these Adja-Yorùbá related groups. Together, these closely related groups accounted for almost half of the original African population on the island alone.

From the Adja-Yorùbá syncretism, Cuba saw the birth of the Afro-Cuban religion known as *santeria* (equivalent to the *candomblé* developed in Brazil by the same ethnic group).

## Maní: The Afro-Cuban Fighting-Game

A traditional fighting-game called *maní* was developed in (or brought to) Cuba by African slaves. Most authors accept that it is of a Kongo-Angolan origin. Nevertheless, despite the possibility that the name could have been created by Bantu speakers – a common form of cultural syncretism which is strongly present in the Afro-Americas – I would like to offer another plausible hypothesis: The *maní* was very popular in the Matanzas province of Cuba, where Yorùbá and Adja slaves were taken in greater numbers than slaves of Kongo-Angola origins. Perhaps both *santeria* and *maní* are a result of the Adja-Yorùbá culture.

Cuban ethnologist-anthropologist and poet Lydia Cabrera, an authority on Afro-Cuban culture and religion, described a game of *maní*, where she states that both "Kongos and Ararás (the Adja-Yorùbá people) were *maní* enthusiasts." She wrote:

> *Peoples of different "nations" gathered around the games of maní, and they were played throughout the island. They appealed to members of both races, as did the revolting cockfights, "and not just ordinary people came to watch the games, but also respectable whites." They bet money on the aggressiveness and fists of the maniceros, just as they bet on the spurs of the fighting cocks. Many women, who were equally strong as the men, also took part in the game, delivering punches that injured their best competitors.*

> *In the Mercedes Carrillo sugar mill, where the Kongos and the Ararás were maní enthusiasts, Micaela Menéndez broke the jaw of a huge man with one powerful blow.*[9]

Esteban Montejo, born as a slave in Cuba in 1860, recollects the fighting-dance *maní* in the nineteenth century, in an interview with Miguel Barnet for his book *The Autobiography of a Runaway Slave*. Coincidence or not, Montejo's father was a Yorùbá man from Oyo, Nigeria:

> *I don't know whether it was really a dance or a game, because they punched each other really hard. This dance they called the maní, or peanut dance. The dancers formed a circle of forty or fifty men, and they started hitting each other. Whoever got hit went in to dance.*

*They wore ordinary work clothes, with colored print scarves round their heads and at their waists. [...] The men used to weight their fists with magic charms to make the maní blows more effective. The women didn't dance, but stood round in a chorus, clapping, and they used to scream with fright, for often a Negro fell and failed to get up again. Maní was a cruel game.*[10]

Ned Sublette expresses doubt regarding the real origin of *maní* while describing another dance, called *columbia*, which was probably inspired by *maní,* and which could have originated in Cuba with Kongo-Angolan roots:

*The dance of the columbia is acrobatic and mimetic, in which one dancer follows another, each trying to outdo the others. It seems to derive at least in part from a pugilistic competition of slavery times, possibly of Gangá and possibly of Congo origin, called maní.*[11]

However, Fernando Ortiz argues for the influence of the Gangá slaves from Sierra Leone and Liberia on both the *columbia* and the *rumba.* In other words, as speculative as it may be, these new Adja-Yorùbá hypotheses are to be carefully evaluated.

## The English/British Slave Trade

The British transatlantic slave trade, which flourished from the mid-seventeenth century until the early nineteenth century, when slavery was abolished in 1807, was a major carrier of Africans to the Americas. Between 1656 and 1807 over three million Africans were transported as cargo to the Americas in British slave ships.

Records indicate that the English started transporting slaves from West Africa to the Americas in 1556, but they engaged in the large scale slave trade in the mid-seventeenth century, and in the third quarter of the century they were dominating the Atlantic slave trade. Records from 1556 to 1810 account for 3.2 to 3.4 million slaves transported as commodity cargo by English (later British) slave traders.

Between 1661 and 1760, over 2,500 slaves were taken to Brazil, mostly to the states of Bahia, Pernambuco and Rio de Janeiro, in eight to ten voyages from the Bight of Biafra, Bight of Benin, Gold Coast, Gulf of Guinea and Senegambia.

The Royal African Company was a slaving enterprise established by the merchants of London and was led by James Stuart, Duke of York, who was King Charles II's brother and later became James II of England and James VII of Scotland. The profits created from slaving in West Africa, particularly in Guinea, helped them export gold to the English mint.

Chartered in 1672, the Royal African Company had the monopoly on English trade to West Africa, which lasted until 1698. The monopoly was extended from Salé (Sallee) (in present-day Morocco) to the Cape of Good Hope (present-day South Africa), with its headquarters located in Cape Coast (present-day Ghana). The company continued to engage in the slave trade until 1731. It was replaced by the Company of Merchants Trading to Africa in 1752. However, private traders, who had been taking part in the Atlantic slave trade since the end of the sixteenth century, long before the company had been established, officially entered the trade in 1712.

The Royal African Company traded mainly for gold, ivory and slaves (the majority of which were sent to English colonies in the Americas, including the mainland). The Royal African Company also maintained many forts and factories in other locations such as Senegambia, Sierra Leone, Upper Guinea, the Windward Coast, the Gold Coast, in Ophra and Whydah (Oidah), the Slave Coast, the River Gambia (James Island), Benin, Calabar and Angola, sometimes very near Dutch and Danish forts.

Most of the British African forts were bought or seized from other European powers in the region and rebuilt or reformed, but they also built forts in Dixcove, Sekondi, Accra, Princes Town, Apam, Anomabu, Mouri, and Whydah, among other garrisons, lodges and trading posts. Fort Metal Cross, originally built by the English in 1691 in Dixcove, and Fort Patience in Apam, originally built by the Dutch, were all chosen as World Heritage Sites by UNESCO.

Cape Coast Castle, originally built by the Swedish and later conquered by the Danish, was seized by the British in 1664 and, for over 200 years, became the headquarters of the British Gold Coast.

The British transported slaves from Africa to North America, the Caribbean Sea islands, and South America, but it was on the U.S. mainland that they established several settlements and delivered most of their cargo of slaves.

## The British Colonies in the Caribbean Sea

Saint Kitts, or Saint Christopher Island, was the first official British colony in the West Indies, established in 1623 (and which would later be divided with the French, who also established a colony in 1625) for the production and exportation of tobacco and sugarcane. The British built Fort Brimstone, which is the present-day Brimstone Hill Fortress National Park, and which is also a UNESCO World Heritage Site. The fort began to be built by African slaves around 1690, and the island alternated political control between the French and the British until 1793. St. Kitts and its close neighbor Nevis were an important route for the English and Dutch ships in the West Indies during their expeditions to Africa on the way to the U.S. mainland. Nevis, which together with St. Kitts forms present-day Federation of Saint Kitts and Nevis, became an important producer of sugar for the British Empire in the early eighteenth century.

Besides St. Kitts and Nevis, from 1623 the British controlled a vast area of the West Indies and the Caribbean Sea, namely the islands of Anquilla, Antigua, Barbuda, Barbados, the British Virgin Islands (Anegada, Jost Van Dyke, Tortola and Virgin Gorda), Dominica, Grenada, Jamaica, Monserrat,

Saint Lucia, Saint Vincent and the Grenadines, Trinidad and Tobago, British Guiana (on the northern coast of South America, the present-day country of Guyana), and British Honduras, which was located on the east coast of Central America, and which is the present-day country of Belize.

African slaves and sugar plantations were present in most of the British settlements, as were slave rebellions, such as the ones in Jamaica, Barbados, British Guiana, Antigua and Granada. Maroon communities also existed in the British domains, and some were of great importance for our approach to the geographically larger notion of the African American Africanism and the preservation of African cultures during and after the slave trade and the colonial Americas. Let's take, for example, Jamaica. According to historical sociologist Orlando Patterson, "with the possible exception of Brazil, no other slave society in the New World experienced such continuous and intense slave revolts as Jamaica."[12]

Jamaica was taken by the English from the Spanish in 1655. It already had a population of black slaves originally from Africa and African descendants. During the British rule, Jamaica became a leading exporter of sugar, and slaves continued to come on a regular basis from different slave ports of West and West Central Africa: Senegambia, Sierra Leone, Gold Coast, Bight of Benin, Bight of Biafra, the islands of the Gulf of Guinea, the Windward Coast, Gabon, Kongo and Angola.

Like the Brazilian experience, the British also brought to Jamaica slaves from the ports of Loango, Malembo, Cabinda, and Ambiz, which, together with Luanda and Benguela, were important suppliers to Brazil from the region made up of Gabon, Kongo and Angola.

## British Slave Rebellions

The slave Maroon rebellions in Jamaica generated more than eighty years of conflicts with the British. As with the Brazilian *quilombos* – a phenomenon which started early in the sixteenth century – the runaway slaves of Jamaica escaped to the mountainous region of the island, called Cockpit Country. Orlando Patterson explains that the first Maroon war began with the conquest of Jamaica from the Spanish by the British in 1655 and lasted for eighty-five years, to 1740, if we include all periods of skirmishes.

Where slaves could be somewhat organized, there were Maroon communities during the whole period of the enslavement of Africans in the Americas, whether in the isolated Brazilian *mocambos*, in small bands, or in the larger communities, such as the centralized state of Palmares and the Maroons of Jamaica.

Like Ganga Zumba and Zumbi dos Palmares in the Quilombo dos Palmares, the Maroons of Jamaica under British rule also had their leader, known as *Captain Cudjoe*, who was from an African Akan origin.* On March 1, 1738, a treaty between the Maroons and the British – known as Articles of Pacification with the Maroons of Trelawney Town – was signed. The treaty, which contained fifteen articles and included Captain Cudjoe's brothers (Captain Accompang, Captain Johnny, Captain Cuffee and Captain Quaco), ended the First Maroon War in Jamaica.

## The British Colonies in the United States

As seen before, the British brought nearly three million slaves to the Americas, bringing close to 300,000 slaves to the U.S. mainland, from the sixteenth to the nineteenth century, the great majority of which were brought to South Carolina and Virginia – the earliest settlements.

---

*His sister, "Nanny of the Maroons," also became an important leader of the Jamaican Maroons worthy of note, in that she was also known for her *obeah* religion – which was culturally closely related to the Adja-Yorùbá *candomblé* of Brazil.

Slave rebellions also took place in the U.S. In South Carolina, for instance, where slaves worked mainly on the rice plantations, under horrible, inhospitable conditions, in 1739 an Angolan (or perhaps Congolese) slave named Jemmy led a small group of slaves near the Stono River to a rebellion that would end in the death of several white and black men during the brief, two-day conflict.

In Virginia, several rebellion attempts took place in the mid-sixteenth century; in 1800, led by Gabriel Prosser; and in 1839, led by Nat Turner.

From the early seventeenth century to 1865, over 100 slave conspiracies, revolts, or conflicts took place in the continental United States of America, mainly in Louisiana, Florida, South Carolina, Virginia and New York. Yet, we shall see why the U.S. became the country with the least level of africanization and the one with the least African cultural components in contemporary times.

## Obeah: Adja-Yorùbá Influences in British Americas

*Obeah* practices have been observed in the British colonies of the Bahamas, Antigua, Barbados and Jamaica since the seventeenth century, "when the colonies became the first in the region to establish slave-dependent sugar plantations."[13] Most of the British slave voyages started in the Bight of Benin and Bight of Biafra combined, from which, among other ethnic groups such as the Igbo, Edo, or Ijo, the great majority were of Yorùbá and Adja (Ewe and Fon) origins (what I term "Adja-Yorùbá"). More than a third of all slaves transported by the British came from these two regions alone.

David Eltis remarks that the seventeenth-century Jamaica, where *obeah* had a strong presence in black society, had two core cultures, the southern English and the Akan/Adja.[14] Paul Oliver explains that "the Adja are closely related to the Akan and Ewe of Ghana,"[15] and authors J. Andrew Grant and Fredrik Söderbaum state that the three groups, the Adja-Fon from Benin, the Yorùbá from southern Nigeria and the Akan from Ghana also had a historical business relationship.[16] Nevertheless, the British Gold Coast was the second most important source of slaves for the British traders and the Adja-Ewe was among the ones embarked from its ports to the British colonies.

## The French Slave Trade

Estimates say that France took from 1.3 to 1.6 million slaves from Africa. More than one million were taken to the Caribbean. Smaller cargoes of slaves were taken to the Spanish Americas and to the American continental lands, through the ports in the Gulf Coast, and to Brazil.

As with the Dutch, France also tried to establish their domains in Brazil, through the *France Antarctique* invasion in 1555 in Rio de Janeiro, which lasted for a little over ten years, whose domain ranged mainly from the coast of Rio de Janeiro to Cabo Frio. In 1612, in the northeast region of Maranhão, another invasion known as the *France Équinoxiale* lasted until 1615, when the French founded the city of Saint Louis, present-day São Luís, after Saint Louis – Louis IX of France – in honor of King Louis XIII.

The French "experimented" with the slave trade still the sixteenth century, but it was only in the seventeenth century, with the acquisition of Saint Domingue (present-day Haiti), that they rose as important players in the slave markets, through their monopoly *Compagnie des Indes Occidentales,* and later the *Compagnie du Sénégal,* being the last European nation to officially engage in this lucrative merchant activity. Although France's trade was mainly to her own colonies in the French West Indies, there were over 4,000 voyages from Africa to the Americas under the French slave flag from the sixteenth century to the mid-nineteenth century.

The French were active in the "triangular trade," through which the European slave ships left Europe for Africa transporting goods such as tools, rum, weapons, and textile products to be exchanged for slaves, who were then transported to the Americas as cargoes to be sold to the planters. The profit from the sale of the slaves was then used to purchase tropical tobacco, coffee, cotton, sugar and molasses for Europe, where they were processed and transformed into goods. There were two types of triangular trade: the European, with its end points in Europe, West and South Africa and the West Indies, and the North American, its end points being New England, The West Indies and West and South Africa.

Brazil had in common with France the use of the West, West Central and Southeast African slave force in their sugar plantations, though it outnumbered France and all the other European nations in the total trade of slaves in the New World. Slaves were transported by the French mostly from the Bight of Benin (Dahomey) and from Angola (Malembo, Cabinda, Ambriz, Dande) and Loango, present-day Republic of Congo (they even had two ships named after the region, *Princesse d'Angole* and *Princesse de Cabinde,* which took slaves to Saint Domingue and Martinique in the eighteenth century), as well as from other slave ports in West Central Africa, Senegambia (Gorée Island), Bight of Biafra, Golf of Guinea, the Windward Coast, the Gold Coast, Sierra Leone, and also from the islands in the Indian Ocean in Southeast Africa. Slaves were shipped to the French colonies in the West Indies and the Caribbean Sea, such as Saint Domingue, Guadeloupe, Martinique, Granada, as well as to South America, in the French Guiana, Rio de La Plata, Brazil, St. Kitts, and to Central America; to Cuba, Jamaica, Antigua, Puerto Rico, the Gulf Coast of the United States, to Georgia in the North American mainland, Tobago, Dutch Guiana, Dominica, Bahamas, and to the Danish West Indies.

You can visit some of the African French forts built during the Atlantic slave trade, such as Fort d'Estrées, built in the 1850s on the north side of Gorée Island, Senegal. It now houses the historical museum of Gorée; the building is a UNESCO World Heritage Site.

In the Gambia, Albreda is just a short walk from the historic village of Juffure – where Kunta Kinte was held as a slave in Alex Haley's famous novel and TV series, *Roots*. Albreda became a French trading post in 1681 and now is a fishing village nestled among tall native trees, with ruins of a slaving station on the banks of the Gambia River, and a small museum dedicated to the history of slavery.

## The French Quilombos

The "French" Maroons also gathered in bands to escape to inaccessible areas of interior forests and establish permanent communities. These types of escapes were known as *grand marronage*, as opposed to *petit marronage*, which described short periods of escapes. This reunion of ethnic groups and cultures in the French Americas unquestionably brought rich traditions to the New World, such as the French Creole architecture of the Mississippi Valley and Louisiana, where there are some beautiful surviving examples; the rich and beautiful Creole cuisine; and the Creole religions, music and dance.

These expressions were originally influenced by Europeans and had French or Spanish "flavor" that was eventually mixed in the new Caribbean rural and urban settings. However – and despite the African origins of this new "black America," and of artistic and cultural expressions such as the *ag'ya*, the fighting-game from Martinique, or *maní* from Cuba – we will gradually see, along this unpretentious literate historic journey, why capoeira was born in Brazil.

## Ag'ya, Chatou, Kalinda, Kenbwa and Vodou

The majority of Africans transported by the French to their colony of Martinique came from the Bight of Benin (Yorùbá and the groups known as

Arada, or Allada, Adja, Adja-Fon, Adja-Ewe). According to David Geggus, slaves imported from the Bight of Benin accounted for 46.4 of the total, compared to 27.1 of slaves from West Central Africa, i.e., Kongo-Angola region.

In 1936 American dancer-anthropologist and choreographer Katherine Dunham traveled to Jamaica, Trinidad, Cuba, Haiti and Martinique – where she filmed performances of the fighting-game called *ag'ya* (or *ladja*), which she later described as "an acrobatic dance that much resembles the Dahomean thunder dance." Slaves from Dahomey were in its great majority from the Adja-Yorùbá groups.

Her celebrated videos show impressive similarities with the old traditional Brazilian capoeira (known as "Capoeira Angola"). However, observing from a martial art perspective – and comparing to capoeira – these similarities end where the complexities and perfect precision of the movements begin.

In Dunham's beautiful short videos, for instance, we can see the awkward and clumsy attempts to deliver *armadas* (the traditional spinning outside crescent kick in capoeira) and *queixadas* (the outside front crescent kick). Several other elements of capoeira are present, although in a very rudimentary form, such as the *negativa* (the dodging ground technique), the *benção* (the straight front heel kick), the *martelo* (the roundhouse kick), and even a rather well done *ponteira pulada* (the jumping front snap kick), a form of *ginga* (the stance, basic footwork movement of capoeira) and music (without a *berimbau*). The "ground navigation," one of the beauties and a distinctive quality of capoeira, is merely a resemblance of the Brazilian art form. Most moves seen in the videos are not sufficiently effective to consider the *ag'ya* a martial art.

We also find in Martinique (as well as in Guadeloupe), the *kenbwa*, or *quimbois*, the equivalent to *santeria* in Cuba, and *candomblé* in Brazil, another Adja-Yorùbá heritage. Several sources agree that the *kenbwa* can be considered a close relative to *obeah* from Jamaica (and other British colonies), which was probably introduced by the Akan (Ashanti) and the Adja, with whom they had a historically strong cultural link. In Saint Domingue, the richest colony of the French colonial empire, slaves from the Bight of Benin, again from the Adja (Adja-Fon) groups, created the system of beliefs and rituals equivalent to the Cuban *santeria* and the Brazilian *candomblé,* known as *vodou,* which was later imported into Lousiana in the United States, where it is still called voodoo.

Guadeloupe also had a traditional fighting-game, or fighting-dance, called *chatou.* In 1949, philosopher and existentialist Jean Paul Sartre witnessed a performance. Would the *chatou* observed by Sartre be the equivalent of the *ag'ya* of Martinique? He wrote:

> *On Guadeloupe, like on Martinique, there is a traditional fight with accompanying songs and beating of drums. This entertainment is called "chatou," a name that means a kind of octopus in Creole, and it is practiced mostly at funeral wakes.*[17]

David Geggus explains the process of acculturation among slaves from different ethnic groups, notably from the Adja-Yorùbá and "Kongo" groups, which may have impeded the preservation of Bantu heritages in the French colonies. The author seems to agree with Herbert Klein, who states that the predomination of one given cultural expression, such as the cults *candomblé,* *santeria* and *vodou,*

> *... had more to do with the history of local acculturation than with the weight of numbers. Thus a small initial group often established the basic cults which later massive migrations from entirely different areas in Africa adopted in their environments.*[18]

On this process of acculturation in the French colonies, Geggus concludes:

> *Several factors may have impeded the preservation of Bantu traits in the French colonies. The age and sex ratios of the West Central Africans were less favorable to the preservation of native culture*

*than those of peoples from the Bight of Benin. The latter's numerical predominance early in St. Domingue's history, as Sidney Mintz and Richard Price argued, perhaps gave them a critical edge in determining the shape of creole culture.*[19]

## Kalinda: Stick-Fighting and Dance in the Caribbean

*Kalinda*, or *kalenda,* is the traditional term for a stick-fight from Trinidad (as well as for the Caribbean and Lousiana dance performed without the sticks). According to Maureen Warner-Lewis, the name has a Bantu origin, though Courlander finds it similar to *susa*, a fighting-dance related to the Adja of Togo.

Stick-fighting was found all over ancient Africa much before the colonial period, therefore it would not be strange to identify more than one ethnic group attached to a version of this combat game. For instance, while Warner-Lewis indicates that *kalinda* is an art with Congolese and Mbundu roots, the beautiful oil painting entitled *A Cudgelling Match between English and French Negroes in the Island of Dominica* – painted by Agostino Brunias around 1779 with a smaller version located at the National Library of Jamaica and a larger version, at the John Carter Brown Library at Brown University – offers a different perspective. The larger painting shows two slaves stick-fighting on the island of Dominica (which lies between Martinique and Guadeloupe): an "English Negro" against a "French Negro." The painting shows one of two things: The creolization and acculturation observed by Klein and Geggus, as the two men are performing the *kalinda*, regardless of their original ethnic groups; or it shows Yorùbá slaves wearing their typical *kafo* pants and head ties (as perhaps an improvised traditional *kufi* hat), playing the Adja stick-fighting version observed by Courlander. In the picture, two men also wear a kind of bowler hat which was also common among the Yorùbá starting in the eighteenth century.

Sources place the origin of the *kalinda* in the French West Indies, from where it was imported to Louisiana as a "voodoo dance," probably from Saint Domingue. It was performed as a male mock combat dance-fight and stick-fighting in Trinidad and in Martinique. Some sources believe it came from the Guinea region, while others believe that it originated in West Central Africa. Courlander's suggestion that it belongs to the same category as the *susa* places its origin in the Adja peoples who were imported by the French from the Bight of Benin (see the Dutch Slave Trade).

Guadeloupe, Saint Domingue and Martinique saw thousands of Nègres Marron slaves from different ethnic groups, such as the Angolans in Guadeloupe and the Yorùbá in Saint Domingue, take refuge in the hills and remote plains of the islands, in Maroon villages similar to the Brazilian *mocambos* and *quilombos*.

# The Dutch Slave Trade

The Dutch explored the Gold Coast for the first time in 1596. During the sixteenth century, their participation in the Atlantic slave trade was not as systematic as it would come to be during the seventeenth and eighteenth centuries, especially after the founding of the Dutch West India Company in 1621, when the Dutch were officially granted the monopoly over the slave trade with the Americas and West Africa, breaking Portugal's monopoly.

However, the Dutch slave trade was not as small as one may believe. Although less important than the commerce of Portugal, France and England, the Dutch slave trade was larger then those of Spain, Denmark, Sweden and Germany. Over 500,000 slaves were taken from Africa, mostly to the Caribbean region, and around 10 percent of those to Brazil and the Spanish Americas.

Slaves were taken mainly to the Dutch Guiana, to Pernambuco in the northeast of Brazil, and to Rio de Janeiro, in the southeast. However, the Dutch traders also carried slaves to North America and to the Spanish Americas, including Dutch privateers who captured slaves from Portuguese ships to sell to the Spanish. Soon the Dutch would become the main suppliers of slaves to the plantations of the Spanish Americas and, for almost seventy years during the seventeenth century, they would constantly take slaves to the northeast of Brazil.

The Dutch slave trade was vital for the emerging Caribbean plantation economies that supplied Europe with valued agricultural commodities such as sugar, cotton and tobacco. Besides their great interest in ivory and in the gold from the Guinea (the Dutch Gold Coast, present-day Ghana), before engaging in the trade of slaves, with the expansion of the sugar commerce in Europe, the Dutch turned their rudders to Brazil in the early seventeenth century.

Pernambuco was the port of entrance of most of the slaves taken to Brazil by the Dutch, who were increasingly interested in the commerce of sugar produced in the country at the *engenhos* (mills), notedly those of Bahia and Pernambuco. As a consequence of its successful financial and maritime expansion, the Dutch sought to control the international supply of sugar and decided to establish their own colony in Brazil by taking over Portuguese possessions by force. Their first attempt occurred in Bahia in 1624, although the Dutch were expelled by the Portuguese one year later. The second attempt came in 1630 in Pernambuco, which was a success and lasted for a total of twenty four years, until they were expelled by the Portuguese in 1654 – but not without taking their knowledge of the operation of the sugarcane mills with them to the Antilles, with the help of Jewish merchants who controlled part of the sugar exportation market (the Sephardim accounted for almost half of the population of Recife at that time).

Sugar was a highly valuable and profitable product in Europe – as was brazilwood in the beginning of the Portuguese colonization period – and had been cultivated by the Portuguese in West Africa as early as the fifteenth century. During the Dutch rule of Brazil, favorable political and geographical climates, as well as less social and religious oppression, attracted Jewish entrepreneurs (Sephardim and New Christians) who had been having a good relationship with Amsterdam, and who partly controlled the production of sugar in West Africa, after introducing new techniques of sugarcane cultivation to the Atlantic islands of Madeira, the Azores, the Cape Verde Islands, and São Tomé and Príncipe in the Gulf of Guinea, and in the sixteenth century to the Caribbean Islands. The Jewish prospered as financers and brokers of the sugar industry and the slave trade (as slaves were the most important laborers of the sugarcane plantations).

## The Dutch Sugar Industry

The Dutch also brought slaves to Brazil and the West Indies from the same regions previously explored by the Portuguese in Africa, such as Elmina (which they conquered from the Portuguese in 1637), in Ghana, and Luanda, in Angola, and were pioneers in improving sugar production in the region. The Dutch West India Company seized and controlled the richest sugar-producing area in Brazil, in the state of Pernambuco, from 1630 to 1654. Dutch sugar enterprises in Brazil served as models for other large-scale French and English Caribbean ventures. Dutch settlers, in fact, introduced sugarcane and the process for making it to the lower West Indies in the early 1600s, and Dutch merchants controlled the copper trade that supplied plantation boiling houses with kettles and boilers.

By the late seventeenth and early eighteenth centuries, the Dutch had become the wealthiest European trading nation to navigate the Atlantic, relying on modern systems of credit, insurance, and finance – until the British challenged them during the second half of the eighteenth century.

After the Portuguese–Dutch war over the control of Brazil, won by the Portuguese, there was increased religious pressure on the Jews, and many of them moved to the Caribbean islands following the Dutch, who were tolerant of religions and now historically related to the Jewish people. This exodus of Jewish people helped establish sugar plantation in the Caribbean islands, and the Dutch became opportunistic "middle men," supplying Caribbean sugar producers with slaves, capital and skills, and supplying Europe with sugar.

After 1675, and until the early eighteenth century, there was great expansion in sugar production by European colonial powers such as France, England and the Netherlands, which helped increase the slave price for the plantations and decrease the sugar quotation in the European markets. This dramatically reduced the profits of the sugar plantations in Brazil, whose sugar hegemony had already been lost to the Caribbean after 1645 and the final departure of the Dutch in 1654.

Nowadays, Brazil is by far the largest producer of sugarcane in the world, with an estimated production of six hundred million tons in 2009.

## Dutch Guiana's Maroons: The Bush Negroes

Slave resistance also happened in the Dutch Guiana (present-day Suriname), where the Maroons were called "Bush Negroes," also known as Djukas. In the entire Caribbean region, resistance helped keep alive the African fight for freedom and for their artistic and cultural expressions, dances, languages, food, craftsmanship, religion, family and companionship. The colony of Dutch Guiana was also developed as a slave-based sugar economy, just like the Brazilian experience, and where the "Bush Negroes" could develop distinctive societies reflecting cultural blending and adaptation to the new local social and political conditions.

However, regardless of the similar conditions that existed between the Dutch and the Brazilian colonies, the fieldwork research on African retention of cultures of the "New World Negro," by Anthropologist Melville Jean Herskovits, which was carried out in Dahomey, Dutch Guiana, Haiti, Trinidad, Brazil, and in the United States – in addition to the work of sociologist Robert Ezra Park – leads us to a broader perspective on the different levels of Africanism in these peoples.

Herskovits recalls that, in the United States, African religious behavior did not follow the same patterns of the Caribbean islands and Brazil and had to be reinterpreted "in terms of a new theology." Herskovits discusses whether the descendants of African slaves have retained Africanisms in their cultural behavior:

> *It is quite possible on the basis of our present knowledge to make a kind of chart indicating the extent to which the descendants of Africans brought to the New World have retained Africanisms in their cultural behavior. If we consider the intensity of African cultural elements in the various regions north of Brazil [...] we may say that after Africa itself it is the Bush Negroes of Suriname who exhibit a civilization which is the most African . . .*

> *Next to them, on our scale, would be placed their Negro neighbors on the coastal plains of the Guianas who, in spite of centuries of close association with the whites, have retained an amazing amount of their aboriginal African traditions, many of which are combined in curious fashion with the traditions of the dominant group.*

> *Next on our scale we should undoubtedly place the peasants of Haiti . . . and associated with them, although in a lesser degree, would come the inhabitants of neighboring Santo Domingo. From this point, when we come to the islands of the British, Dutch, and (sometime) Danish West Indies, the proportion of African cultural elements drops perceptibly . . . though . . . we realize that all of African culture has not by any means been lost to them.*[20]

In his field research, Herskovits found that many ancestral African customs existed among the Bush Negroes, who, because of their long isolation from the coastal regions and the settlements (much like the *palenques* and *cumbes* of the Spanish Americas and the *quilombos* of Brazil, or the settlements of the *grand marronage* in the French possessions), had experienced minimal contact with Europeans.

Park argued that the way in which the black slaves were distributed was also responsible for their kind of adaptation and acculturation.

Nevertheless, a dance-fight in a ring made of people clapping and singing to its music was never recorded in the Dutch Americas before the Dutch invaded Brazil in the seventeenth century. In this vein, it is interesting to contrast the *maní* and the *ag'ya,* which were mentioned earlier, with the capoeira from Brazil in order to establish their unique cultural patterns.

Today the remains of most of the early European and Dutch forts and slave ports can be visited, such as the House of Slaves, on Gorée Island, in Senegal; James Island in the Gambia River; Fort São Jorge da Mina, or St. George d'Elmina, at Elmina Beach; Fort St. Anthony, built by the Portuguese and later modified by the Dutch; Fort Batenstein, built in 1656 in Ghana; and castles and slave ports in several points of West Africa, mainly in Ghana. UNESCO has declared most of these sites as World Heritage Sites of immeasurable historical importance. The island of Arguim, off the coast of Mauritania, where slaves were sent to Portugal as early as the mid-fifteenth century, is also a UNESCO World Heritage Site, as part of the Banc d'Arguin National Park, for its breeding site for migratory birds.

## Susa and Obeah in the Dutch Guiana

According to Patrick Taylor, "*susa* is a special ceremonial dance related to ancestral spirits and links directly to the head spirit,"[21] but Harold Courlander, in Rhoda Lois Blumberg's *Black Life and Culture in the United States,* tells us that among the dance songs of the Djukas there was a fighting-dance called *susa* which is used for competition, that the dance is related to a type which is found among the Ewe of Togo (i.e., the Adja-Yorùbá), and that its description suggests that it also belongs to the same category as the *kalinda*,[22] which brings us the doubt about the real origin of the latter.

According to Margarite Fernández Olmos and Lizabeth Paravisini-Gebert,[23] the practice of *obeah* was also found in the Dutch Guiana, which strengthens the hypothesis of an Adja origin due to their large geographic and ethnological proximities with the Akan (Ashanti), especially if we assume that the *kenbwa* from the French Caribbean is in fact a close relative to the Jamaican *obeah*.

# The Danish–Norwegian Slave Trade

The Kingdom of Denmark–Norway entered the Atlantic slave trade in the second half of the seventeenth century, after the European profits in Africa triggered their interest in the Atlantic trade. After the success of its European neighbors in Africa, Copenhagen was ready to follow suit.

At first, gold, ivory and palm oil were their main goal, which was soon followed by the more lucrative business of the slave trade.

The Danish Gold Coast (a.k.a. Danish Guinea) settlements were established as early as 1658 in present day Ghana, lasting until 1680 under Danish control, when it was sold to Britain. The empire built its first stronghold on the coast, Fort Fredriksborg, in 1660, close to Cape Coast Castle in Ghana. In 1661 another fort had its first lodge constructed at Osu, a district of Accra, in Ghana, by the Swedish, which became the Christiansborg Castle (now also known as the Osu Castle) until it was seized by the Dutch and later by the Danish. Apart from several trade posts along the coast of present-day Ghana and Togo, the Danish–Norwegian empire built Fort Fredensborg in 1736, some 75 kilometers from Fort Christiansborg; Fort Kongensten, in 1783, in Ada, around 110 kilometers east from Accra; and Fort Prinsensten, 1784, in Keta, around 185 kilometers east of Accra, in the Volta region.

In the Caribbean Sea, the Danes settled on the island of St. Thomas around 1670, and in early seventeenth century on the islands of St. John and St. Croix. They were known as the "Danish West Indies" and were exploited by the Danish West India Company, which administrated the islands until 1754, when the government took control. These three small Caribbean islands – the present-day United States Virgin Islands – were, for a good two hundred years, a Danish–Norwegian colony.

Before the abolition of slavery in 1848, the population of black slaves on the three islands altogether outnumbered that of the white, free people.

Around 80,000 slaves were taken from Africa and brought mainly to the Danish West Indies to work in the plantations. Over 15 percent perished during the voyages – a common number for all European slavers.

An interesting historical event took place in Fort Christiansborg. In 1786, after spending three years in the post, German scientist Paul Erdmann Isert, chief surgeon appointed to the Danish mission, participated as a physician aboard the slave ship Christiansborg, which departed from Guinea to the Danish West Indies. On the second day at sea, he witnessed a slave rebellion. The 452 African slaves (with approximately 160 men) rose against the whites, which resulted in the deaths of 34 slaves and the wounding of 2 crew members. He visited the West Indies before returning to Fort Christiansborg.

Isert sought to end the slave trade by trying to establish productive plantations on African soil with the help and the association of the native African people. He wrote a series of letters to his father in which he accounted for the inhumane treatment of the African natives and the mistake that was slavery. Isert not only established a successful experience in the village of Akropong, named Frederiksnopel, but he also registered the will of the slaves to organize rebellions against the horrors of slavery – a pattern that was repeated during most of the over 400 years of African-Atlantic slavery and under all slave ship flags.

Paul Erdmann Isert and his family were killed three years later at Christiansborg, presumably by those who were against the idea of ending the slave trade. His accounts demonstrate the feasibility of partnership between the African peoples and the Europeans on colonial soil.

The Osu Castle can still be seen in front of Labadi Beach, in Accra, as well as the ruins of the other Danish forts in Ghana.

In 1768 the Norwegian slave ship Fredensborg sank in a storm off the coast of Arendal, in Norway. The wreck was found by Leif Svalesen and a team of underwater archaeologists and divers in September 1974, in a remarkable discovery, in the outport of Narestø, a location which caught the world by surprise. The region has preserved some interesting landmarks, such as a slave ship captain's house, on the island of Merdø, the Merdøgaard Museum, an annex of the Aust Agder Museum, where the maritime declaration was held after the Fredensborg was wrecked on the island of Tromøy; and the Tromøy church in Merdøgaard.

## The Slave Rebellion of St. John

The Danish slave rebellion of St. John was one of the longest in the history of the Atlantic slave trade. Some sources acknowledge that slaves from the Akwamus tribes of Ghana on St. John could not see themselves as slaves, because, historically, these warriors were slave owners in Africa. Many were of royal families and wealthy merchants, and most were used to internal tribe wars in Ghana. Other sources state that the leaders of the rebellion were the Mina slaves, equally fierce and resistant warriors from Ghana. However, consistent sources state they were in fact the same, i.e., the Akwamus were part of the Forest Akan speakers who were labeled as "Mina" due the broad historical geographic reference of Costa da Mina (the Mine Coast), as the

Gold Coast was called by the Portuguese, and from where these slaves embarked to the Danish West Indies.

The St. John slave insurrection started on November 23, 1733, when the slaves revolted against the owners and managers of the island's plantations. The slave rebellion was one of the earliest and longest slave revolts in the enslaved Americas, during which the insurgents captured the fort in Coral Bay and took control of most of the island. The revolt ended in May 1734, after six months, when troops sent from Martinique finally defeated the insurgents.

# The American Slave Trade

In 1526, Spanish explorer Lúcas Vázquez de Ayllón, while on an expedition to the eastern coast of the United States, made landfall in present-day South Carolina. He arrived with a cargo of horses, supplies and 600 people – including 100 enslaved Africans brought from San Domingo, Hispaniola – and founded the infamous colony of San Miguel de Gualdape.

There are unofficial accounts of African slaves in Spanish Florida as early as the mid-sixteenth century, much before the English colonization of North America in the state of Virginia, in 1607. Records are imprecise; some account for the first landing of African slaves in Virginia taken by a Dutch ship in 1619, an English ship in 1628, or another Dutch ship to New York in 1655. Ayllón could have been the first to take slaves to mainland America, as early as 1526.

The first African slaves imported directly from the Kongo and Angola regions of West Central Africa and taken to the North American mainland, arrived in Jamestown, Virginia, on a Dutch ship in 1619. They were probably captured from a Portuguese slave ship and taken to the slave markets of Virginia, where they were sold, perhaps to work on the tobacco plantations.

They were part of a large trading system originally established by the Portuguese in Africa, which included the capture and supply of slaves to the Spanish colonies in the Caribbean, Central and South America.

Soon, history was repeated, and the Virginia planters increasingly had to rely on more slaves from Africa. By the mid-seventeenth century, there was a large demand for African slaves in Virginia, and slave ships began to arrive more frequently.

Slaves were first in demand for the tobacco plantations, such as the ones in Virginia, and rice, further south in South Carolina and Georgia. The typical American plantations would use small groups of slaves, ranging generally from 10 to 30 individuals. This contrasted sharply with the Brazilian sugar plantations, which often used more than 100 slaves – and on some farms, nearly 300 – in the factory's several production processes, as well as with life at the *engenhos de cana de açúcar,* the Brazilian sugar mills.

Due to the large extension of farmlands in Brazil and the increasing demand for more sugar, the need for new arrivals (and great quantities) of slaves from Africa was constant, lasting for over three and a half centuries. In 1600, only one hundred years after the official discovery of Brazil, the population of black slaves and descendants was four times the population of white Europeans and European descendants. This created an important social phenomenon, as the new Brazilian population – an identity still to be formed – began very early to be stratified into "whites" and "blacks," and not only into "white Europeans masters" and "slaves." Little by little, the Africans and the new Afro-Brazilian people began to rise in cultural importance, and, eventually, to influence the white minority still searching for their own identity.

On the other hand, slave communities in the United States were much smaller and scattered in their geographic distribution. On many of the American farms, notably the ones with a low death rate, the slave population was able to reproduce and grow on its own, without new infusions from the Atlantic slave trade. This particular phenomenon is of great importance when we compare the modus operandi of Brazilian and American slavery and the effects of the Afro-acculturation of the two regions.

For instance, "Brazilian" slaves could also reproduce and grow on their own; however, since the very early times of the Atlantic slave trade, they could preserve their African seeds, i.e., slaves were born in an African or Africanized ambience. It is wrong to reason that the first black slave communities in Brazil were the *quilombos* and *mocambos;* these were actually the result of their very first communities, which began as soon as a sizeable group of slaves got together for a reasonable period of time, regardless of their status, whereas on American soil slaves who did not form a community were eventually blended with the local communities, first by gradually absorbing their share of the new American, regional way of life.

Later, cotton and sugar plantation owners could count on the early "tobacco experience" and spread their production from Virginia to the southern regions of the U.S. By the end of the nineteenth century, now under U.S. rule, the state of Louisiana, with its nearly 2,000 plantations, had already seen the largest slave revolt in the American history, the 1811 German Coast Uprising. The revolt was triggered by slaves from the sugar plantations at Côte des Allemands, a settlement above New Orleans in the Mississippi River parishes of St. Charles and St. John the Baptist, where German settlers had established residence in the early eighteenth century.

Although estimates of the total number of slaves involved in the revolt vary from 100 to 500, this event still did not specifically contribute to the formation of an "Africanized nation" of blacks in the U.S. as in the Brazilian model. An "African heritage movement" or an "African conscience" would come much later, now at the expense of organized, educated and politicized African Americans.

The U.S. also saw Maroon communities and the alliance with Native Americans, as it was seen elsewhere in the Americas. Fugitive slaves and former members of the defunct Corps of Colonial Marines inherited Fort Gadsden from their British allies after their evacuation from Florida in 1815, joining forces with the Native American Choctaw and Seminole. Hundreds of black fugitives and free people settled in a village protected by the fort, which became known as Fort Negro. Word of mouth rapidly spread, and more fugitives and free people came to settle around the fort.

The British left their post with weapons and ammunition and, as they became organized, the black population, together with their Native American allies, started launching raids into Georgia while controlling peace amongst the surrounding populations. The fort was built near the Apalachicola River, which was a common route to and from Georgia, some 130 kilometers away.

In 1816 a series of battles between the American army and the black rebels ended when the Americans destroyed the fort with heavy artillery, killing hundreds of people inside. The rebellion was over after a battle that lasted for several days.

Presently, Fort Negro is listed in the U.S. National Record of Historic Places and named as a National Historic Landmark.

## American Slave Ships: Small, Fierce Vessels

During the sixteenth century, most slaves from West Africa and West Central Africa were sent to the West Indies, where the demands for slaves was higher. Only in the eighteenth century did the American mainland start to import slaves as a regular and profitable merchant activity.

Nearly 300,000 slaves (other sources account for as many as 600,000) were taken to the U.S. during the slave trade, and approximately 60,000 embarked under the American flag to the U.S. mainland, to the Spanish colonies, and to countries such as Brazil, the Caribbean Islands including the British, Danish and Dutch West Indies, British Guiana, Dutch Guiana, and the French colonies.

The American ships brought slaves mainly from the West Central Africa region, from Gabon, Kongo and Angola, and from West and Southeastern Africa. For instance, slaves coming from the same African ports used by Brazilian importers were traded into the U.S. in the early seventeenth century, as we can read in *Documents Relative to the Colonial History of the State of New-York*.*

In a letter by the Reverend Jonas Michaëlius, of the island of "Manhatas," in "New Netherland," to the Reverend Adrianus Smoutius of Amsterdam, written in August 1628, he says:

> *[...] maidservants are not here to be had, at least none whom they advise me to take; and the Angola slaves are thievish, lazy and useless trash. The young man whom I took with me, I discharged after Whitsuntide, for the reason that I could not employ him out of doors at any working of the land and, in doors, he was a burden to me instead of an assistance. He is now elsewhere at service with the boers.*

No wonder this poor Angolan boy was not very interested in engaging in Mr. Michaëlius's ideas of "assistance." Perhaps the young African was as mischievous and cunning as his counterparts in Brazil, except for the fact that he was alone in a pulsing seventeenth-century New York.

The institution of slavery was a plague per se. But if one considers the rural and urban settings of the African slaves in Brazil, as compared to the same conditions in the U.S., it is easy to conclude that the "American"

---

*Volume II 1858. Page 768. Appendix.

slaves were solitary beings not only in their occasional confinements, as a direct result of cruel punishments, but mainly in their social and emotional confinements, as they were irremediably separated from their kin during the cruel American distribution process.

However, from a more humanistic view, the process a black slave underwent during the enslavement years in the Americas was practically the same, with punishment, poor or insufficient food, mistreatment and indifference. No attention was given to the slaves' health once they were on a plantation, and in rare cases, the slaves could celebrate special religious festivities together for a couple of days.

Through the years, freed U.S. slaves who achieved a better social position would get their own slaves – another situation with parallels in Brazil.

As Junius P. Rodriguez explains:

*Slavery in the United States has traditionally been portrayed as an institution that was based on race. Generally speaking, this conviction is correct, but its propagation has led to the almost universal belief that all slaveowners were white and that all slaves were of African descent. In reality, although there were no white slaves, there were black slaveowners from the colonial period to the Civil War.*[24]

*[...] Black slaveowners, as did white owners, obtained slaves by inheritance, gifts, and purchase.*[25]

The abolition of slavery in the United States came in 1865, 32 years after the Abolition of Slavery Act was passed in Britain and 23 years before the Lei Áurea, the "Golden Law" of abolition in Brazil, was signed in 1888. Like the other nations engaged in the African slave trade, the United States had the same operational method, up to the delivery of their precious cargo, while the distribution of the slaves among the plantations and properties had one basic difference: Often, only a few slaves were sent to each site. Some ships, for instance, would bring as few as ten or twenty slaves. J. Saunders Redding, a black American writer, describes the arrival of a ship in North America in the year 1619:

*Sails furled, flag drooping at her rounded stern, she rode the tide in from the sea. She was a strange ship, indeed, by all accounts, a frightening ship, a ship of mystery. Whether she was trader, privateer, or man-of-war no one knows. Through her bulwarks black-mouthed cannon yawned. The flag she flew was Dutch; her crew a motley. Her port of call, an English settlement, Jamestown, in the colony of Virginia. She came, she traded, and shortly afterwards was gone. Probably no ship in modern history has carried a more portentous freight. Her cargo? Twenty slaves.*[26]

Howard Zinn quotes historic documents in the *Journals of the House of Burgesses of Virginia* of 1619, which tells of the first twelve years of the Jamestown colony. He writes about one of the settlements having one hundred slaves and a limited quantity of food. As more people (slaves) arrived, there was even less food to be divided. He also describes people living in holes, like caves. About the winter of 1609–1610, he wrote, the slaves were

*Driven through insufferable hunger to eat those things which nature most abhorred, the flesh and excrements of man as well of our own nation as of an Indian, digged by some out of his grave after he had laid buried there days and wholly devoured him; others, envying the better state of body of any whom hunger has not yet so much wasted as their own, lay wait and threatened to kill and eat them; one among them slew his wife as she slept in his bosom, cut her in pieces, salted her and fed upon her till he had clean devoured all parts saving her head...*[27]

According to Professor Thomas A. Tweed, of the National Humanities Center at the University of North Carolina, Chapel Hill, a small number of African slaves were Muslim, estimated by some at 10 percent. The majority of slaves brought to America their own beliefs, based on polytheistic religions such as the *candomblé* of Brazil and the voodoo of Louisiana, which sometimes overlapped with animist religions and syncretized with Christianity. Over the years, the new generations would find their own American identity in Christianity, especially through the black churches.

In an article written for BBC News, author Leslie Goffe says that thousands of African Americans are seeking their African roots by means of DNA tests.

Changing a Christian name to a Muslim name is a trend that has grown tremendously among African-Americans, under the assumption that Christian names were slave names given to their ancestors by the slave masters, in the belief that Christianity was used to "perpetuate slavery" and other "injustices against the black people," or simply because one's ancestry came from Muslim Africa. However, the Arab slave trade, which had been going on for centuries before the European slave trade, was active in North and East Africa, and Arab Muslims settled in Africa long before the Portuguese arrived.

David Livingstone describes an expedition commanded by the Portuguese explorer Fernando Barreto, in Southeast Africa, as early as 1569. When the explorers arrived at the Zambezi River, in Mozambique, they found Arab traders already settled in the region:

> *The expedition was commanded by Francisco Barreto, and abundantly supplied with horses, asses, camels, and provisions. Ascending the Zambezi as far as Senna, they found many Arab and other traders already settled there.*[28]

Livingstone also describes an Arab slave party he contacted during his voyage of exploration to East Africa in the nineteenth century, near Lake Shire, in Malawi:

> *[...] a large slave-party, led by Arabs were encamped close by. They had been up to Cazembe's country the past year, and were on their way back, with plenty of slaves, ivory and malachite. In a few minutes, half a dozen of the leaders came over to see us.*[29]

Among other passages, Livingstone accounts for an encounter with an Arab slave trader called Juma ben Saidi, in Nkhotakota (or "Kota-Kota"):

> *He was very busy in transporting slaves across the Lake by means of two boats, which we saw returning from a ship in the afternoon. As he did not know of our intention to visit him, we came upon several gangs of stout young men slaves, each secured by the neck to one common chain, waiting for exportation, and several more in slave sticks.*[30]

Livingstone's accounts indeed show that slavery was a misery of men and not of religion. The following passage puts the Arab slave traders on equal grounds with the Europeans (i.e., Christians) – and, in some cases, even in superior greed, as Livingstone narrates:

> *When we met the same Arabs in 1861, they had but few attendants: according to their own account, they had now, in the village and adjacent country, 1,500 souls.*[31]

## The Swedish Slave Trade

The Swedish were one of the last Europeans to enter the slave trade. The Swedish Africa Company was first chartered in 1649 (controlled by private investors), establishing a base in Cape Coast, Ghana, in 1650. In 1655, under a new charter, the company became controlled by the crown. According to Junius Rodriguez, in 1655, 36 slaves were transported as cargo by the Swedish to the Island of São Tomé to work on the sugarcane plantations. In 1658, 500 to 600 slaves were taken to the island of Curaçao.[32]

There are few records of slave transportation, mostly to the São Tomé island, present-day São Tomé and Príncipe. The company's main interest was in gold, timber and ivory, brought from Africa, and sugar and cotton, which they brought from the plantations in the West Indies, which were sent to Europe. Sweden was one of the producers of the iron chains used to transport slaves from the inlands to the coast. According to Tor Sellström,[33] about one thousand slaves were sold in Sweden brief transatlantic slave trade. The company established forts and lodges in Butre, Anomabu, Takoradi, Benyin and Accra, all settlements in present-day Ghana, in what became known as "the Swedish Gold Coast." Slaves were mainly sold to São Tomé and Curaçao, an island of the Caribbean Sea off the coast of Venezuela, established by the Dutch as a trading settlement in 1634, and which belongs to the Netherlands Antilles. The capital, Willemstad, is part of UNESCO World Heritage due to its historical districts and colonial buildings.

The Swedish West Africa Company was founded in 1649 and in 1650 landed in *Cabo Corso* (Cape Coast). In 1653 they originally built Fort Carolusburg (Carlsborg) in Cape Coast, Ghana, now known as Cape Coast Castle Museum, which has been identified by the UNESCO World Heritage Foundation as a World Heritage Monument. Cape Coast lies 168 kilometers west of Accra.

In 1784, King Gustav III of Sweden negotiated a swap with Louis XIV of France, who received warehouse space in the port of Gothenburg in exchange for the island of St Barthélemy, or St. Barth. St. Barth was officially discovered by Christopher Columbus in 1493, who named it after his younger brother Bartholomew, and had a population of some 700 people, including one-third of this number in slaves. The island had been annexed by the French in 1648. Swedish Saint Barthélemy lasted until 1878, when it went back to French control.

In 1638, the Swedes established their colony near present-day Wilmington, in the state of Delaware. The first expedition consisted of two ships, and landed on March 29. From 1638 to 1655, New Sweden (parts of present day American states of Delaware, New Jersey and Pennsylvania) was a Swedish colony on the U.S. mainland.

The Swedish Gold Coast lasted until 1663, when it was seized by the Danes and integrated into the Danish Gold Coast. During the Atlantic slave trade, Sweden had colonies in the Caribbean islands of Tobago, Guadeloupe and Saint Barthélemy, and on the U.S. mainland, partly partnered with the Finns and the Dutch, in the Delaware Valley, along the Delaware River, which occupied parts of present-day of Delaware, New Jersey and Pennsylvania. Compared to other European traders, few slaves were brought to the U.S. by the Swedes. Swedish trade of slaves was made illegal in 1813 and the abolition of slavery came in 1847.

# The Brandenburger/Prussian Gold Coast

Brandenburg was a historic margraviate, a principality which formed the primary nucleus of the Prussian State. The Brandenburg African Company was created under the rule of the Great Elector of the Holy Roman Empire, Friedrich-Wilhelm von Brandenburg, and its successor, the Kingdom of Prussia. In 1683, a Brandenburger expedition built Fort Großfriedrichsburg (Fort Gross Friedrichsburg) near Cape Three Points, in Ghana, which became the headquarters of the Brandenburgs in Africa. For roughly 35 years the Brandenburgers held sovereignty over several forts as far as on the small island of Arguin (Fort Arguyn), in the Bay of Arguin, present-day Mauritania, which was conquered in 1685; in Takrama; Takoradi; Akwida (Ft. Dorothea);

the Kingdom of Whydah (once Gléwé in the small kingdom of Xwéda), present-day Ouidah; and Princes Town, or Pokesu.

For the triangular trade, Brandenburg-Prussia used the island of Arguim and a part of the island of St. Thomas, in the Danish West Indies, leased from the Danes. The main trading item on the island of Arguim was gum arabic, which was traded along with other merchandise.

## The Junkanoo Festivities

The Junkanoo is a street parade of West African origin that is celebrated on several Caribbean islands. It is performed with music and dance every December 26 and on New Year's Day.

There is strong controversy among historians about the origin of Junkanoo, and many have suggested different roots for this festival. The most accepted one is that the word "Junkanoo" comes from the name "John Conny" (or "Konny," "Kunu," "Connu" – perhaps "John Canoe," due to the fact that the local natives led by John Conny used canoes to fish and transport men and goods along the coast). Being a leader and a merchant, Conny could have been an accomplished fisherman, or managed a fishing fleet along the coastal boundaries of his realm. He was the ally of the Brandenburgers in the Gross Friedrichsburg fort during the seventeenth-century slave trade in the "German Gold Coast." Local African legend in Princes Town says that after John Conny returned to the fort to fight against the Dutch, he was captured and sold as a slave to the West Indies, where he became a legend known as "John Canoe."

John Atkins (1685–1757), a British naval surgeon, during his stop at Cape Three Points on the coast of Ghana, during his 1721 expedition on the Guinea Coast, describes John Conny as a charismatic leader, the chief of Princes Town, who had several wives and good table manners, and who could speak English.

*John Conny himself stood on the shore to receive us, attended with a guard of twenty or thirty men under bright arms, who conducted us to his house.*[34]

In addition to their headquarters, Fort Gross-Friedrichsburg, and to Fort Arguin, a number of small garrisons and forts were established by the Brandenburgers along the coast of the African western region.

Restored Fort Gross-Friedrichsburg, as well as part of the original house where legendary John Conny lived, and where he received John Atkins and his party in 1721, can still be visited in Princes Town, Ghana, which lies 264 kilometers west of Ghana's capital of Accra.

Between 10,000 and 30,000 African slaves were shipped to the Americas by the Brandenburg African Company, which, ultimately, left the Gold Coast in the 1720s.

During the Atlantic slave trade, most slaves were embarked on several points in Senegambia; Sierra Leone; Upper Guinea, or simply "Guinea," also known by its division in the Pepper Coast, or the Grain Coast*; the Gold Coast (present-day Ghana); and the Slave Coast, which comprised what today are the coastal regions of east Ghana, Togo, Benin and Nigeria, from Rio Volta to the Lagos Channel); and the Windward Coast (from Cape Mount, present-day Robertsport and Grand Cape Mount in Liberia, near the border with Sierra Leone in the north, to Assinie in the south, in the present-day Ivory Coast, near the border of Ghana, thus overlapping the Pepper Coast). Part of the region comprising from Cape Palmas to Cape Lopez, in Gabon, is the Gulf of Guinea, where we find the Bight of Benin and the Bight of Biafra

---

*This territory roughly covered the coastal regions of Guinea, Sierra Leone, Liberia and part of the Ivory Coast, approaching the Gold Coast.

(present-day Bight of Bonny) and from West Central Africa (including mainly the Kongo-Angola region).

East Africa's Madagascar, Comoros Islands, Mozambique and Tanzania were also important sources of slaves to the Atlantic routes, though on a lesser scale. They were used to supply labor to the plantations on the islands of Mauritius (Île de France), Reunion and Seychelles, in the Indian Ocean.

# THE CRADLE OF CAPOEIRA

## The Findings of Africa and the Atlantic

As seen earlier, after the conquest of Celta in 1415, the Portuguese were the first Europeans to establish a settlement on the coast of Africa.

### *Romanus Pontifex*

*Romanus Pontifex* is a papal bull written on January 8, 1455, by Pope Nicholas V to King Afonso of Portugal. The bull follows the *Dum Diversas*, of June 18,

Negroes Fighting, Brazils, Augustus Earle, National Library of Australia, ca. 1822.

1452, which had confirmed indefinite powers to King Afonso of Portugal *"to attack, conquer and subdue the Saracens, pagans and other infidels, enemies of Christ, to enslave them and seize their lands and goods."*[35]

The *Romanus Pontifex* confirmed to the Crown of Portugal the dominion over all lands discovered or conquered during the Age of Discovery and it is historically a very powerful document, almost a "property deed," as we can see from the excerpt below:

> *Nicholas, bishop, servant of the servants of God. For a perpetual remembrance.*

> *... granted among other things free and ample faculty to the aforesaid King Alfonso – to invade, search out, capture, vanquish, and subdue all Saracens and pagans whatsoever, and other enemies of Christ wheresoever placed, and the kingdoms, dukedoms, principalities, dominions, possessions, and all movable and immovable goods whatsoever held and possessed by them and to reduce their persons to perpetual slavery, and to apply and appropriate to himself and his successors the kingdoms, dukedoms, counties, principalities, dominions, possessions, and goods, and to convert them to his and their use and profit– by having secured the said faculty, the said King Alfonso, or, by his authority, the aforesaid infante, justly and lawfully has acquired and possessed, and doth possess, these islands, lands, harbors, and seas, and they do of right belong and pertain to the said King Alfonso and his successors ...*

## While in Africa ...

The main industries in pre-colonial Africa were gold mining, iron working, salt making, cloth weaving and other art and craft industries, in addition to agriculture and animal herding.

During the Atlantic slave trade, the Europeans traded, among other products, gold, silver, ivory, pepper, gum arabic, ostrich feathers, ebony, dyewoods, palm oil, nuts, yams, hides, animals, kola nuts, salt, dried fish, iron, textiles, baskets, grains, and, of course, slaves.

## Slavery in Mother Africa

Life of the peoples of ancient Africa also depended on trading, and the large African continent was the place of both the internal trade, which occurred among neighboring settlements, and throughout the coastal areas where, later, slaves from the forest and coastal kingdoms would be the most important goods of the Atlantic slave trade.

Much before the Europeans arrived, different foreign slave trades had already happened in pre-colonial Africa, from where African slaves were sent to the Islamic World, to India or to the islands in the Indian Ocean. East Africa had long seen the slave trade in what would be the European model much before the "European" West Africa saw the birth of the Atlantic slave trade, while the Arab and trans-Saharan trade constituted a traditional commercial route, which had been building the curiosity of Iberian Europe for over a century, long before the Portuguese first conquered the African west coast.

Slavery was an original ancient African institution, and slaves were needed to serve in community and domestic chores, for farming and several of the kingdoms' needs, or to serve powerful members of the tribes. These African slaves could be prisoners of war, people who had committed a crime in their own community, or had an unpaid debt, or perhaps an unlawful sexual relationship with another person, or they could be hunted in other tribes (although mainly for a belligerent reason), sometimes among the same ethnic group, for the specific purpose of serving as slaves.

Nevertheless, the "Arab trade" continued during the European Atlantic slave trade, as we can see from Frederick Freeman's notes:

*A caravan of Moorish merchants arrives, and offers goods for slaves. If there are no slaves on hand they must be procured. The Sultan immediately collects his forces, marches into the country of some harmless tribe, burns their villages, destroys their fields and flocks, massacres the infirm and old, and returns with as many able bodied prisoners as he can seize. Sometimes 3,000 have been obtained in a single "ghrazie," as these expeditions are called.*[36]

# First, the Atlantic Islands

Apart from small rural experiences, which included sugarcane in the Portuguese Algarve and the Spanish Andalusia regions, slavery in Europe was almost an exclusively urban institution throughout the first half of the fifteenth century; therefore, it had very limited importance to the economic environment, as compared to what it would represent during the Atlantic slave trade in the New World.

The enslavement of West Africans for agricultural – thus primarily economical – purposes would only come in the second half of the fifteenth century, when the Portuguese introduced sugar plantations on the Madeira, the Azores and Cape Verde islands, on the island of São Tomé, and when they explored the Canary Islands, which were later conquered by the Spanish, with slaves coming from the ports on the coast of Africa.

This "economic migration" would be responsible for triggering the Atlantic slave trade in the New World, where the Portuguese would establish important advanced posts on their islands on their way to or from Africa and back to Portugal.

These early slaves of the Atlantic islands produced the very beginning of the religious and social syncretism that would later be strong in the Caribbean and especially Brazilian social and cultural settings during and after the

Atlantic slave trade. Some of these slaves had more than one generation of experience with different European settlers, and were more "educated" and "acculturated" before being sent to Brazil and the West Indies.

## The Madeira Islands: The First Atlantic Slave-Sugarcane Experience

The Madeira Islands (present-day Madeira, Porto Santo, Desertas and Selvagens) were officially discovered between 1419 and 1420 by Portuguese navigators João Gonçalves Zarco, Tristão Vaz Teixeira and Bartolomeu Perestrello, who were on a journey to the West African coast. At first, they found land on a small island that they named Porto Santo – the very first of the many discoveries made under Prince Henry the Navigator, although it was believed that the islands had been known before, as both Madeira and Azores appear on a Genovese map of 1351.[37]

Madeira was the first to become the largest producer of sugar in the European merchant circle by the end of the fifteenth century, before the Spanish Canary Islands rose to take its place as the larger source of the product, with São Tomé becoming the last largest producer of all the islands, and the model for the sugarcane plantation system used in the Americas, including relying exclusivly on black slave labor.

Madeira established the standard, the pattern of an island emporium and an advanced trade post for the traders sailing to and from Portugal along the African coast.

## The Azores Islands: Early Slave Revolts on the Rise

We have seen that the first European settlers of the Azores in the early fifteenth century were a mixed group of people, mainly Christian settlers, from several

Portuguese provinces, including Madeira. They were soon joined by black slaves and other Europeans. For this reason, there were many languages spoken on the islands in its early colonization period, but soon Portuguese became the standard language.

After the discovery of the island of Santa Maria, before building settlements, the Portuguese imported livestock to the island to serve as future supply for the settlers. Eventually, villages were built and resources brought to the islands of Santa Maria and São Miguel, where the first plantations of sugarcane were built.

In the beginning, the Azorean colony was an advanced African-Atlantic trade post at service of the mother country, which worked as a station for Portuguese ships to be repaired and resupplied, and as a warehouse of commodities produced on the islands or on African soil. This procedure would come to be adopted on all five Atlantic islands off the coast of West Africa.

## Cape Verde Islands: Future Land of the Batuque

After Venetian explorer Alvise Cadamosto reached Cape Verde in 1456, at service of Prince Henry the Navigator, these islands began to be settled based primarily on the standards set by the settlement of Madeira.

Due to different climate differences – not having a steady tropical climate, such as the one on the island of São Tomé – the sugarcane production did not reach the level that the Portuguese first foresaw for the island. Settlers started to inhabit the islands around 1462 with the help of African slaves coming firstly from the Upper Guinea coast, and later from the more distant Bight of Benin, perhaps through São Tomé, according to Jesuit Alonso de Sandoval (see page 142). Some ten years later, São Jorge da Mina, in Ghana, became one of the most important headquarters of the Portuguese in West Africa, and slaves from this region would also be taken to the main island of Santiago.

Cape Verde was in the confluence of the Portuguese main slavery routes: from São Tomé to Madeira and to Portugal, and from the slave ports on the western coast of Africa to Brazil and to the Spanish Americas. From the late fifteenth century onwards, many slaves captured in the ports that served São Tomé also reached Cape Verde, which, ultimately, became a slave emporium for Africans coming more or less from two large regions: the Gulf of Guinea and Upper Guinea.

However, all the attempts to produce an economically feasible sugarcane production in Madeira, the Canary Islands and on Cape Verde reflected sparse results, which was not the case with São Tomé.

The *batuque* dance form appears to have been born in Cape Verde, or brought to the island of Santiago in the early years of slavery (see Samba: Poetry in the Feet, page 145).

## The Canary Islands: The Successful Spanish Venture

Not only the Canary Islands are said to have been visited centuries before "official" records, but most of the Atlantic islands have similar stories, such as the Genovese map of 1351 showing the Madeira and the Azores islands. Imprecise records indicate that in 1312, a Genovese sea captain called Lanzarotto Malocello landed on the island which is now called Lanzarote. He was followed by other Italian, Portuguese and Spanish sailors, who explored the archipelago. However, according to Charles Verlinden, Malocello probably arrived on the island around 1336, at the service of the Portuguese.*

In the following century, before the islands were definitely claimed by the Spanish, the rival Portuguese imported slaves from the African continent and introduced the sugarcane plantations to the island, after their experience

---

*Slavery of black Africans was recorded by the Kingdom of Sicily and Italy long before the Portuguese and Spanish trade to Europe.

with Madeira; in the early sixteenth century the Canary sugar production became larger than the one of their northwestern Portuguese neighbors, although black slavery on the islands appeared not to have reached the same proportions as that of the Portuguese Atlantic possessions. In 1493, in his second voyage of exploration of the Americas, Christopher Columbus transported sugarcane from the Canary Islands to what is now the Dominican Republic. In 1479 a treaty between Spain (Castile and Aragon) and Portugal sealed the transfer of power over the Canary Islands to the former.*

## São Tomé: The Plantation Model

The island of São Tomé was discovered by the Portuguese explorers João Santarém and Pedro Escobar, somewhere around 1470, as part of the Portuguese maritime plans to explore West Africa and search for a route to "the Indias." The island began to be populated 15 years later by João de Paiva, its first *donatário*, and after some five years began to be settled by Alvaro Caminha, who then became its governor. Caminha introduced the organized slavery system and the sugarcane plantations to the island, with the help of *degredados* (convicted or exiled people), mostly of a large Jewish community, which, according to oral traditions, was composed mainly of children who had been expelled from Spain and Portugal for religious reasons.

At first with a small sugarcane plantation, the excellent tropical climate of the island was an invitation for a much larger scale production, and the African coast, about 299 kilometers from present-day Libreville and 140 kilometers from Port Gentil, made West Africa an easy source of slave labor, although sources indicate that the first slaves on the island were the Adja-Yorùbá from Benin.

---

*See VERLINDEN, Charles (1958), *Lanzarotto Malocello et la découverte portugaise des Canaries.*

Still in the late fifteenth and in the sixteenth centuries, São Tomé exported timber – an experience which would be repeated in 1502 in Brazil – and became the largest sugarcane exporter to Europe, in addition to exporting slaves, first to Europe and later to the New World.

# The Ethnic Groups

Many different ethnic groups were brought to the Americas during the slave trade. From Senegambia to South Africa and to East Africa, it is almost impossible to know, precisely, the origins of all groups and languages. Sometimes it is easy to confuse a language or dialect spoken in a region with an ethnic group, or consider a subgroup to be major ethnic group, such were the quantity of migrations all over Africa. For instance, the Bambara is related to the Mandinka, while both are large ethnic groups that belong to the major Mandé ethnic group; the Ewe and Fon are related to the Adja people, who are also related to the Yorùbá; the Mina could be slaves from the Akan and the Yorùbá and Adja cultures – just to mention a couple of examples.

Some authors consider mutually intelligible languages as branches of the same ethnic tree; however, there are dialects which are spoken by a broader range of society in a given geographic area, despite the fact that not all speakers belong to the same ethnic branch. During the slave trade, the Europeans found a profusion of dialects spoken in the many kingdoms and societies during the period of the slave trade.

## *Peoples and Names*

There is also great confusion regarding the names of ethnic groups, or subgroups, as they were called by their main traders. Again, just to consider some examples, on a geographic approach, with some of the names by which these ethnic groups or subgroups were known, they are (without absolutely trying to exhaust the subject):

The Fula (Fulani, Peuhl) peoples of Mauritania, many of whom were also present in most of West Africa, from Mauritania to Cameroon, including Mali, Burkina Faso, and in Chad, Sudan and present-day Central African Republic; the Songhai of Mali; the Wolof (Jola) people who inhabited Mauritania, the Senegambia and present-day Guinea Biassau, as did the Balantas and the Manjagos (Manjack, Manjaku, Manjaco), who also inhabited the Gambia; the Fulani (Fula, Peuhl) of Guinea; the Mandinka (Malinke, Mandé and Mandingo), who represent a large group of ethnic groups who inhabited the Gambia and most of West Africa, including the Bambara, among others; the Temne people of Sierra Leone; the Kpelle (Guerze) and the Bassa (Bantu) peoples of Liberia; the Akan (Ashanti, Asante) people of Côte d'Ivoire and Ghana; the Ga-Dangme people of Ghana; the Adja speaking peoples: Adja, Fon and Ewe, and the Yorùbá (Jeje) people of Ghana, Togo, Benin and Nigeria; the Igbo, Igala, Efik, Ibidio, Annang, Gwari, Itsekiri and Urhobo and the Ijo (Ijaw) peoples of Nigeria; the Edo, or Bini people of the Benin Kingdom (Nigeria); the Bantu speakers of the Duala (Douala), Bulu, Bassa and the Beti-Pahuin peoples of Cameroon; the Fang (Bantu) people of the Spanish Guinea (present-day Equatorial Guinea) and Gabon; the Mpongwe (Bantu) of Gabon; and all the Bantu peoples of west central, south and southeast Africa, including present-day Congo, Democratic Republic of Congo, Angola (Cabinda), Namibia and Mozambique (this is a rough reference, as many of these ethnic groups, who were a majority in a kingdom, could also belong to another kingdom as part of a large group, or as a minority).

## The Findings of Brazil

According to documents at IBGE (Brazilian Institute of Geography and Statistics), in 1491, nine years before the official discovery of Brazil by Pedro

Alvares Cabral, Portuguese people lived in brick houses on Itamaracá Island, in the state of Pernambuco. Homero Fonseca explains, although he states that he did not find historical evidence:

> *Reports without historical evidence, as this one recorded at the IBGE indicate the presence of shipwrecked Portuguese and French pirates on the island of Itamaracá even before the official discovery of Brazil. The report informs the names of two Portuguese – João Coelho da Porta da Cruz and Duarte Pacheco Pereira – as having been in Brazil respectively in 1493 and 1498.*[38]

However, for some historians, there is little doubt that Duarte Pacheco Pereira had visited Brazilian lands before Pedro Alvares Cabral. In *A Construção do Brasil* (The Construction of Brazil, Lisbon, 1995), Portuguese historian and professor Jorge Couto supports the thesis of the discovery of Brazil in 1498 by Duarte Pacheco Pereira based on his research of the original manuscript *Esmeraldo de situ orbis*,* written by Duarte Pacheco between 1505 and 1508, which was missing for nearly four centuries before being published in Portugal.

Regarding the discovery of Brazil, the manuscript presents information in its second chapter of the first part, in the following concise passage:

> *As in the third year of your reign of the year of our Lord one thousand four hundred and ninety-eight, where your Highness had us discover the lands towards the west, going beyond the vast ocean sea, where it is found and navigated a very large mainland, with many adjacent large islands, very populated, running from seventy degrees north of the equator to twenty eight and a half degrees south of the same equinoctial circle.*[39]

If indeed Pacheco arrived in Brazil before 1500, African slaves and Creoles may have reached Brazil coming directly from Portugal to Pernambuco in the late fifteenth century. Pacheco, who had complete knowledge of the

---

*Lisbon, Imprensa Nacional, 1892.

Treaty of Tordesilhas, was a rich explorer who had traveled along the West African coast and visited the islands of Cape Verde, where slavery had been established in the fifteenth century, and many Portuguese were accustomed to travel with fairly educated slave servants during these North Atlantic voyages.

## First Slaves in Brazil

Officially, Portuguese colonists and merchants brought the first African slaves to Brazil in 1549, fifty seven years after Columbus landed in Hispaniola.

According to different sources, Brazil received six to eight million slaves from the various parts of West Africa, West Central Africa and South and Southeastern Africa, as we have seen earlier. From primitive tribes to more advanced civilizations, different ethnic groups from distinct and sometimes distant geographic regions were taken during the Atlantic salve trade. They were brought to work on sugarcane, coffee and tobacco plantations and in gold and diamond mines; to ranch cattle and work on small crops; to attend to domestic chores; and to build churches and construct roads, paving the way to the start of the Brazilian colonial infrastructure.

However, the African slave rebelled since the very early times of the Atlantic slave trade. Many revolts began while still on the slave ships, and slave rebellions continued to exist throughout the entire slavery period in the New World, regardless of ethnicity.

Historian Petrônio Domingues tells us that

*since the beginning of slavery the black population has shown certain capacity to organize collectively.*[40]

Citing Artur Ramos in *O Espírito associativo do negro brasileiro,* Domingues explains:

*The trajectory of the Black population in Brazil was marked by the spirit of racial unity. Until the abolition, there were organized socio-economic, religious and ludic groups and associations of black people, which were represented by comradeships, religious fraternities, candomblés, congada festivities, cash loans and manumission councils, batuques, singing, capoeira groups, quilombos.*[41]

The author adds other collective social-cultural manifestations such as *moçambique, lundu, jongo, maculelê* and the "secret societies."

## Slave Revolts

John Atkins, an eighteenth-century British naval surgeon who traveled onboard a slave ship to Brazil and the West Indies, describes captive Africans who rejected food during a crossing, which was seen as a form of resistance, or perhaps because these slaves were depressed. Atkins describes how they were forced to eat:

*The common, cheapest, and most commodious Diet, is with Vegetables, Horse-Beans, Rice, Indian Corn, and Farine... This Food is accounted more salutary to Slaves, and nearer to their accustomed way of Feeding than salt Flesh. One or other is boiled on board at constant times, twice a day, into a Dab-a-Dab (sometimes with Meat in it) and have an Overseer with a Cat of-nine tails, to force it upon those that are sullen and refuse.*[42]

Alexander Falconbridge, another British surgeon who served on slave ships during the Atlantic slave trade, wrote in 1788:

*When the negroes, whom the black traders have to dispose of, are shewn to the European purchasers, they first examine them relative to their age. They then minutely inspect their persons, and inquire into the state of their health; if they are afflicted with any infirmity, or are deformed, or have bad eyes or teeth; if they are lame, or weak in the joints, or distorted in the back, or of a slender make, or are narrow in the chest; in short, if they have been, or are afflicted in any manner, so as to render them incapable of much labour; if any of the foregoing defects are discovered in them, they are rejected. But if approved of, they are generally taken on board the ship the same evening. The purchaser has liberty to return on the following morning, but not afterwards, such as upon re-examination are found exceptionable.*[43]

*The traders frequently beat those negroes which are objected to by the captains, and use them with great severity. It matters not whether they are refused on account of age, illness, deformity, or for any other reason. At New Calabar, in particular, the traders have frequently been known to put them to death. Instances have happened at that place, that the traders, when any of their negroes have been objected to, have dropped their canoes under the stern of the vessel, and instantly beheaded them, in sight of the captain.*[44]

Falconbridge left us a remarkable legacy of records on the customs and practices of the slave traders; from their ports of origin in Africa to the slave ships, and on to their ports of entry in the Americas, African-enslaved Africans were examined with a severity not usually seen when cattle ranchers evaluate their livestock for commercial purposes.

*There is great reason to believe, that most of the negroes shipped off from the coast of Africa, are kidnapped. But the extreme care taken by the black traders to prevent the Europeans from gaining any intelligence of their modes of proceeding; the great distance inland from whence the negroes are brought; and our ignorance of their language (with which, very frequently, the black traders themselves are equally unacquainted) prevent our obtaining such information on this head as we could wish...*

*While I was in employ on board one of the slave ships, a negroe informed me, that being one evening invited to drink with some of the black traders, up on his going away, they attempted to seize him. As he was very active, he evaded their design, and got out of their hands. He was however prevented from effecting his escape by a large dog, which laid hold of him, and compelled him to submit. These creatures are kept by many of the traders for that purpose; and being trained to the inhuman sport, they appear to be much pleased with it...*[45]

*It frequently happens, that those who kidnap others, are themselves, in their turns, seized and sold. A negroe in the West Indies informed me, that after having been employed in kidnapping others, he had experienced this reverse. And he assured me, that it was a common incident among his countrymen.*[46]

# The Quilombos: Resistance and Social Placement

One of the theories advocates that the eighteenth century was really the cradle of capoeira. Incidentally, according to Mestre Acordeon (Bira Almeida), it was in the eighteenth century that the name "capoeira" was associated for the first time with the Brazilian martial art-game.[*]

Slaves, who had revolted and escaped their shackles in the sugarcane mills of Pernambuco, hid in the wilderness in organized and rather large inland communities of black fugitives and other minorities, which were later

---

[*]ALMEIDA, Bira (United States, 1986), *Capoeira, a Brazilian Art Form: History, Philosophy, and Practice*, pp. 17.

known as *kilombos* in the Kimbundu language, one of the Bantu languages spoken in Angola, and referred to as *quilombos* in Portuguese.*

The runaway slaves, called *quilombolas*, were politically, militarily and commercially active, with knowledge of diverse agricultural methods, hunting, fishing, craftsmanship, metallurgy and administration, which they had inherited from their ancestors. It is said that theft from outside the *quilombos* was also one of their economic activities.

The most famous *quilombo* is the Quilombo dos Palmares, in the Capitania de Pernambuco, a settlement some historians agree had more than 50,000 runaway or former slaves by 1670, including some aborigines and Caucasians. This *quilombo* was situated in the present location of the state of Alagoas, in northeastern Brazil, which, still in the seventeenth century, came to be an illegal but powerful independent state.

Ganazumba – "The Great Lord" in *mbundo,* or Ganga Zumba, as he is known in Brazil – was the first leader of the Quilombo dos Palmares and was considered a king by the other leaders of the *mocambos*, the smaller settlements that evolved within the larger *quilombo*.

However, Ganga Zumba, despite the Bantu origins argued in most Brazilian texts, which include the terms *quilombo* and *mocambo*, was probably from an ancestral Adja-Yorùbá lineage, as Robert Nelson Anderson III, professor of Portuguese and Latin American Studies at the University of North Carolina, explains:

> *Ganga-Zumba was probably the title rather than the proper name*
> *of the king or paramount chief of Palmares in the 1670s. However,*
> *it probably does not mean "Great Lord," as is often rendered in the*

---

*In Africa, the *kilombos* were temporary prisons, which served as trading posts for African people captured by other Africans and were known in Angola in the sixteenth century at the beginning of the European transatlantic slave trade. According to official Brazilian records, in 2006 there were more than 3,500 communities originating from the first *quilombos* throughout Brazil, with an estimated 1.7 million descendants of the original *quilombolas*.

*Portuguese sources. Nganga a nzumbi was a religious title among the Imbangala whose responsibilities included relieving sufferings caused by an unhappy spirit of a lineage ancestor (nzumbi). In a fundamentally lineageless society like the Imbangala – or the colonial Maroon – this official would have great importance, as it would fall to him to appease ancestral spirits cut loose from descendants who would otherwise propitiate them. Despite the title and apparent official function of Bantu origin, the Ganga-Zumba known to history was possibly a native Palmarino of the Ardra Nation, identifiable with the Ewe-speaking Allada state on the Slave Coast.[47]*

In 1677 Ganga Zumba defeated the Portuguese troops led by expeditionary Fernão Carrilho to Palmares, which increased the efforts of the Portuguese authorities to propose an agreement and stop the slave rebellions.

Ganga Zumba was finally convinced to make peace with the Capitania de Pernambuco in 1678, when he signed with Portuguese Governor Pedro de Almeida the treaty that would give him and his followers the region of Cucaú, where they, as well as any newborn in their land, were to be free, as long as they left Palmares on condition that runaway slaves from outside Palmares and Cucaú would be sent back to their masters.

The treaty with the Portuguese governor was considered inadequate by the other leaders of the *quilombo*. Oral traditions say that Ganga Zumba was killed as early as 1678 by supporters of his nephew, Zumbi dos Palmares, a prominent leader of the *quilombo* himself, who opposed the treaty and remained in divided Palmares with his loyal followers when Ganga Zumba left with his people for Cucaú.

As we can infer from Robert Nelson Anderson's article, the name "Zumbi" is most probably a corruption of "Nganga a nzumbi," i.e., "Ganga Zumba," which corroborates his thesis.

Nowadays there are historical debates as to whether Ganga Zumba was a traitor or a heroic diplomat for his people. Similar treaties had been successful in other countries of the Americas, and Ganga Zumba probably knew that his heavily fortified kingdom, known as the Republic of Palmares, would not last very long.

Most likely due to the lack of consistent documented history, Zumbi and the Quilombo dos Palmares take most of the credit for the development of capoeira in Brazil.

In 1655, twenty-three years before Ganga Zumba perished, a newborn baby, probably taken from one of the captured slaves from Palmares, was given to a Portuguese Catholic priest, Father Antonio Melo, of Porto Calvo, a district of the Capitania de Pernambuco that bordered Palmares.

Father Melo baptized the boy with the name Francisco and gave him a Catholic education, teaching him Portuguese, Latin and religion. When Francisco was 10, Father Melo made him an acolyte of his church. When the boy turned 15, he ran away to Palmares, where he would later become the legendary Zumbi and lead his people in the struggle against slavery.

Notwithstanding what has already been said and written about the Quilombo dos Palmares and how it has been representative of capoeira, some additional light can be shed on the subject through a more liberal analysis of the slave trade in Brazil.

African slaves never gave up fighting against slavery. Available historical records from the seventeenth century, which contribute to the greater expression of the Quilombo dos Palmares, all but reinforce the suggestion that these rebellions were shaped long before that, as early as the sixteenth century, when the slave trade began in the Americas.

There are some contradictions about the official date of arrival of the first African slaves in Brazil. Some historians say that Portuguese explorer and aristocrat Duarte Coelho, who was the first *donatário* of the Capitania de

Pernambuco, brought the first slaves to Brazil around 1539. Another widely accepted theory is that Portuguese merchant of *pau-brasil* Jorge Lopes Bixorda brought a cargo of African slaves from Guinea to Bahia in 1538. However, writings of Francisco Adolfo de Varnhagem, the Viscount of Porto Seguro, suggest that in 1531 Martin Afonso de Souza disembarked in Bahia some slaves found in the caravel *Santa Maria do Cabo,* which was then seized and incorporated into his fleet.

Nevertheless, long before construction of the *engenhos* commenced in Brazil in 1533, several *feitorias* of *pau-brasil* had already been established in the regions of Pernambuco, Bahia, Rio de Janeiro and São Vicente, from around 1501 to 1516.

## Building the Unique Brazilian Identity: The Abolition

Brazil had the longest period of African slavery in the history of the Atlantic slave trade. Although the abolition of slavery came under the *Lei Aurea* (the "Golden Law") only in 1888, Brazil had already signed a treaty with Great Britain prohibiting the slave trade on November 7, 1831; three subsequent regulatory laws passed, the final one on November 14, 1850. The treaty was a direct result of the first convention signed between Portugal and Great Britain, which was confirmed by the Emperor of Brazil (then a sovereign nation independent of Portugal) in 1826, and was ratified in London in 1827 as the first steps toward total abolition. During this hiatus of over twenty years, the slave trade continued at full speed.

This British–Portuguese–Brazilian treaty gave the British Empire special powers to supervise the compliance with the agreements and suppress the slave trade. Selected slave-trade treaty committees were formed by the British, and the captains of the British ships started sending reports to these committees on suspected transportation of slaves. On December 31, 1852, Commander G. D. Keane, on board of the ship H. M. S. *Grecian*, wrote the authorities of an American slave ship, the *Camargo*, in Quelimane, Mozambique – officially the last slave ship to land saves in Brazil – with a cargo of some 500 to 600 enslaved souls who were "delivered" in Rio de Janeiro:

> *During the last six months there have been few vessels met with; none of those appeared to be engaged in slave trade; they belong to Mozambique, and trade with the different ports within the Portuguese territories.*
>
> *I, however, boarded in October a Portuguese brig ("Sublima") from Lisbon, bound to Mozambique, and although I found nothing that would warrant her detention, yet from her general appearance I strongly suspect she will embark slaves should the opportunity be afforded her. In June last the American brig "Camargo" arrived off Quillimane, having on board M. Azaredo, a merchant of that place; she was bound to Mozambique, and I believe proceeded to that port; her movements since are uncertain, but it is reported that in November last she left the Maindo River (73 miles south of Quillimane) with from 500 to 600 slaves on board.*[48]

On a dispatch from Her Majesty's Commissioners at Cape Town, dated March 31, 1853, signed by the Earl of Clarendon, the destiny of the ship is revealed:

> *Although considerable numbers of negroes have been collected at the usual places on the coast, we have not heard of any vessel which has succeeded in evading Her Majesty's cruisers, and carrying off a cargo of slaves, except a vessel which was on the coast under American colours, as the "Camargo." This vessel we learned shipped her cargo of slaves just above Quillimane, and landed them near Rio de Janeiro.*[49]

There was another American ship that transported Africans to Brazil later, in 1855, however unsuccessfully. The schooner, *Mary E. Smith*, also known as "the last slave ship to Brazil," left Boston in 1855 destined for the coast of Espírito Santo, where it arrived in January 1856, carrying 400 blacks who had been captured and bought in Africa. However, both the cargo and the crew were captured by the Brazilian authorities.

During the Atlantic slave trade, the biggest diversity of enslaved peoples from Africa were transported to Brazil, mainly to the coasts of Pernambuco, Bahia and Rio de Janeiro, and large populations of slaves were continuously being thrown in the rural and urban settings of the country almost up to the end of the nineteenth century, when slaves, manumitted slaves and free men would coexist with peoples from different cultures and civilizations, as well as with new generations of African descendants, Creoles and mulattoes, with *bozales* and *ladinos* slaves, including those who were trying to reach the more privileged condition of "*ladino*," and people who could not reach this status.

## The Distribution of Slaves in Brazil

Reviewing some historical facts, Brazil was a colony of Portugal between 1500 and 1822. In the first years of colonization, the main economic activity was the extraction of brazilwood, the "*pau-brasil*" (*Caesalpinia echinata*) which yielded a valuable red dye, whose hardwood is ideal for making bows for stringed musical instruments. The *pau-brasil* was obtained primarily through trade with the indigenous population, which was partly enslaved, and later, as of 1534, from the work of African slaves.

During the colonial period, the Portuguese administration was characterized by the goods being demanded in Europe, and the production potential offered by the new colony. In 1504, following the successful experience of the Infante D. Henrique on the Madeira Islands in 1433, the first *capitania hereditária* (hereditary captaincy) in Brazil was given to Fernão de Noronha, who had the concession to explore for *pau-brasil* in the colony. However, Noronha did not show interest in the island, and it was only in the early 1530s that a system of *capitanias hereditárias* was established by the Portuguese crown, dividing the new colony into fifteen stretches of coastal land, from north to south, each under the rule of an appointed *donatário*, or *capitão-mor*, whose power was very ample. The system of captaincies was terminated in 1821.

After the early "brazilwood cycle," the Portuguese – and the Dutch, during their brief period in Brazil – inaugurated a sequence of new colonial cycles at distinct historical periods and geographic locations, which involved the production of various commodities that were exported to Europe. The most important were the cycles of sugarcane, gold and diamonds, rubber, tobacco, cocoa, cotton, and coffee, among others.

Slave societies grew in Brazil, at first, wherever there were extractive economic activities, mainly those meant for export. A few decades into the slave trade, steady groups of slave populations could be found all around the country, which included several generations of Brazilian-born slaves. Slave hands were used in the construction of urban centers and the slave – and freed black – population was soon integrated into the country's urban settings.

From our historical perspective, the major areas of slavery and slave trade were: Pernambuco, the heartland of the colonial sugar industry in colonial Brazil; Bahia, with the production of sugar and tobacco; Rio de Janeiro, as the fastest growing city and with the production of *cachaça* (the most popular distilled alcoholic beverage in Brazil, made from fermented sugarcane) and the production of sugar in the north of the state, and coffee; and Minas Gerais, for the mining of gold and diamonds, for cattle ranching and the cultivation of coffee, with slaves coming mainly from the northeast, the southern provinces and Rio de Janeiro.

Before other urban centers became largely populated, Recife, which, due to the Dutch invasion of Brazil became one of the most cosmopolitan cities of the world; Salvador, the first colonial capital of Brazil; and Rio de Janeiro, the new capital (from 1763 to 1960) and the most populous city in the second half of the seventeenth century, had become important commercial, cultural and political centers.

The others were Maranhão, Pará, Santos (São Paulo also had large sugarcane plantations and produced *cachaça*, as in the neighboring Rio de Janeiro), and the south of Brazil, represented by Rio Grande do Sul, where slaves worked mostly with livestock; Santa Catarina, where they worked on small crops and livestock; and Paraná, generally coming from São Paulo to work in the gold mines and in agriculture and livestock. These slave populations focused mainly on the internal or local economy, and the majority was initially imported from the northeast; however, several sources show that the internal migration of these populations worked on both sides, with slaves coming from the northeast regions to the southeast and to further south and vice versa, according to the regional economic status of the moment.

Slaves were employed in urban tasks such as constructing buildings and streets. In his fabulous collection published in 1834, French painter Jean Baptiste Debret depicted the slaves making a street in Rio de Janeiro, published in his *Voyage Pittoresque et Historique au Bresil* (A Picturesque and Historic Voyage to Brazil). Scarce historical sources suggest that the high number of manumissions was partly responsible for the constant flow of African and Afro-Brazilian people into the Brazilian markets, as well as for the preservation of Africanisms and its introduction to the urban settings in Brazil, and the preservation of their mythical links with Africa.

On the one hand, as a parallel to the rest of the enslaved Americas, small runaway slave settlements in Brazil also did not function as headquarters or triggers for slave rebellions, but rather as a means to sustain themselves. On the other hand, due to the extent, variation and the internal movement of slaves who were sold to other states, Africanisms could be more freely expressed in Brazil during the years of the slave trade and slavery in the country. As we have seen earlier, the type of distribution of slaves would play an important role in the future socialization and acculturation of these slaves in their new rural and urban settings.

In his interesting works on this subject, Dr. Rafael de Bivar Marquese, professor of History at the University of São Paulo, explains:

> *Firstly, we must compare the economic weight of the indigenous population in central Spanish America against the generalized use of slaves in Portuguese America. Secondly, we can contrast the lack of economic integration among the colonies of Spanish America with the very respectable integration (for the means of transportation of the period) that mining brought to the Portuguese colony, from Rio Grande do Sul in the south to Pernambuco up north – despite the deep rift between the Amazonian valley and the rest of Brazil. Thirdly, and most importantly, the transatlantic slave trade played a crucial role in fuelling economic growth in Portuguese America. And here is a point of substantial divergence with the French and British colonies, where the slave trade was always controlled from the respective fatherlands. In Portuguese America, from the beginning of the 17th Century, the slave trade was organized directly from the Brazilian ports, that is, the large slave dealers that ensured the supply were actually based in Recife, Salvador and Rio de Janeiro, rather than in Lisbon.*[50]

Marquese also brings us some reflections on a text written in 1838 in the north of the state of Rio de Janeiro (my translation):

*I have seen slaves who were slave masters, with plantations, cattle breeding and horses, owners of large and profitable estates. I've seen many slaves earn their freedom, become large landowners, being sodiers, making to senior officers, and serve other public offices of great importance. So many officials and members of even higher orders were, at another time, slaves, and are now living with their families, working for the good of the State in the works and jobs that they occupy, increasing the population and the splendor of the nation which has naturalized them!*[51]

*Without slavery, what would be of America's export trades! We need slaves to work in the mines and obtain this precious metal so much desired, those diamonds that have been such a great resource to the State; this profitable and above all interesting crop, the main wealth of Brazil, and of America in general, which Europe itself can no longer ignore. It is the slave that makes up most of the crew of our vessels, which supply our port cities with goods from the other provinces, so that in a country so extensive and so deserted, it is highly expensive to find free men to hire as sailors. These reflections would lead me too far, and would need a pen even more fruitful than mine, so I will transcribe a passage from a French author which will serve to prove what I mean above.*[52]

Mary Karasch concluded that Rio de Janeiro received more diversified groups of slaves who came from West and East Africa,[53] with which Luís Carlos Soares agrees, adding that "there is no doubt that this ethnic diversity – much larger than that which existed in Salvador and in the Recôncavo Baiano, its hinterlands – influenced the cultural and populational formation of Rio de

Janeiro in a much different way than we have seen in the capital of Bahia and its surroundings."[54] On another note, he reminds us that the degree of ability of the different African ethnic groups to adapt to the new life in the colonial Brazil "could have varied from nation to nation due to the fact that these different groups had other forms of social and cultural organizations."

## African Dances and Fighting Dances

Benjamin Latrobe was a British-born architect, civil engineer and naturalist who traveled the United States during the late eighteenth century and early nineteenth century. Among other works, Latrobe is known for the design of the United States Capitol and the Baltimore Basilica. In his 1905 *The Journal of Latrobe: The Notes and Sketches of an Architect, Naturalist and Traveler in the United States from 1796 to 1820,* Latrobe recalls his impression of a dance he attended in New Orleans, a former French colony in the U.S., to where many slaves had been sent from Dahomey and the West Indies. Latrobe describes several elements that were present in similar cultural expressions of all the enslaved Americas, notably as of the mid-eighteenth to nineteenth centuries:

> *The music consisted of two drums and a stringed instrument. An old man sat astride of a cylindrical drum, about a foot in diameter, and beat it with incredible quickness with the edge of his hand and fingers. The other drum was an open-staved thing held between the knees and beaten in the same manner. They make an incredible noise. The most curious instrument, however, was a stringed instrument, which no doubt was important from Africa. On the top of the finger board was the rude figure of a man in a sitting posture, and two pegs behind him to which the strings were fastened. The body was a calabash. It was played upon by a very little old man, apparently eighty or ninety years old. The women squalled out a burden to the playing, at intervals,*

*consisting of two notes, as the negroes working in our cities respond to the song of their leader. Most of the circles contained the same sort of dances. One was larger, in which a ring of a dozen women walked, by way of dancing, round the music in the center. But the instruments were of different construction. One which from the color of the wood seemed new, consisted of a block cut into something of the form of a cricket bat, with a long and deep mortise down the center. This thing made a considerable noise; also a calabash with a round hole in it, the hole studded with brass nails, which was beaten by a woman with two short sticks. A man sung an uncouth song to the dancing, which I suppose was in some African language, for it was not French, and the women screamed a detestable burden on one single note. The allowed amusements of Sunday have, it seems, perpetuated here those of Africa among its formers inhabitants. I have never seen anything more brutally savage and at the same time dull and stupid, than this whole exhibition.[55]*

Perhaps Latrobe watched the *yanvalou* (the dance of the knees), or the *zepòl*, as it is called in Haiti. This dance is described by Jacques Roumain in his book *Le Scrifice du Tambour* (1943) as a ritual dance from Dahomey. Melville Herskovits and Katherine Dunham trace its origin to the Fon people (Adja speakers); in her book *Island Possessed,* she describes *yanvalou* as "The Arada-Dahomey vaudum cult rhythm and dance," and *zepaules as* "a ceremonial dance with accent on shoulder movements."[56] According to Gerdès Fleurant, the *zepòl,* known as "the dance of the shoulders," is the fastest version of the *yanvalou,* where the performers move their shoulders back and forth during the dance.[57] Yolande Behanzin Joseph-Nöel tells us that this kind of dance was to be found in other U.S. states, such as New York and New Jersey, confirming its Adja origin.[58]

Moreau de Saint Méry and Warner-Lewis relate another Afro-Caribbean creolized dance, known as *chica*, to the *kalinda* danced in Lousiana, to which

Warner-Lewis relate the *bélé* danced in Dominica.[59] According to Behanzin Joseph-Nöel, there were several forms of *kalinda* in the Americas. Actually, there is evidence of slight differences in just two kinds of styles: the *kalinda* "dance" (without sticks), and the stick-fighting, in which the sticks are called *bois*.

Forms of tribal dancing as part of rituals and festivities, such as the *efundula*, the war dances; the dance-drama, such as the *nguni* dance; as well as fighting competitions, including stick-fighting and wrestling, could be found in all of pre-colonial Africa. Jane Plastow's description of the African dance-dramas holds true to help explain the diversity of expressions that existed at the same time in different parts of Africa and in the enslaved Americas:

> *In a multiplicity of manifestations dance drama appears to have originated as an expression of village or clan unit. Although some dances are relevant only to sections of the community, many more included the whole of village society, if not as equal dancers, yet still as a participatory audience which might change roles with performance or musicians. Dancers came together to celebrate community achievements: crop planting, harvest, success in battle, hut building, initiations and weddings.[60]*

In addition, dancing was not a prerogative of one specific ethnic group. African dances were an important cultural expression for a number of reasons. John Atkins describes a dance he saw during his visit to Sierra Leone in the early eighteenth century:

> *Dancing is the diversion of their evenings: men and women make a ring in an open part of the town, and one at a time shews his skill in antick motions and gesticulations, yet with a great deal of agility, the company making the music by clapping their hands together during the time, helped by the louder noise of two or three drums made of a hollowed piece of tree, and covered with kid-skin.[61]*

By comparing Atkin's description of this dance in Sierra Leone with the description of the *efundula* made by Larson in Ovamboland (see page 110), we notice incredible similarities, which confirm that these types of dances were spread across the entire African continent.

Despite the many related festivals, rites and fighting-dances that existed in pre-colonial Africa, these cultural expressions and physical arts were not necessarily ethnically interconnected; in the Americas, for instance, original African elements gave birth to a variety of local cultural expressions such as the Junkanoo, the national festival in the Bahamas, the syncretic religions of voodoo in Haiti and Louisiana, *santeria* in Cuba and *candomblé* in Brazil, the *susa* of the Dutch Guiana, the *ag'ya* dance-fight of Martinique and the martial art of capoeira in Brazil, briefly speaking.

Many of these rich cultural and artistic expressions are preserved and still practiced in their original countries, such as the religious festivities of the Caribbean islands and Brazil, the *susa* in Suriname and the Brazilian capoeira.

During my research to write this book, I contacted several diplomatic entities to try to confirm the existence of these national expressions. All the ones I mention in the book once were, or still are indeed part of these countries' cultural legacies. This was the case with the Embassy of Suriname, to mention one example. I asked if *susa* was, or still is part of their cultural heritage, and I received the following answer from Ms. Hillary de Bruin, researcher, music teacher, singer and Head of the Department of Cultural Studies at the Ministry of Education of Suriname:

> *Susa is a dance of the descendants of the former African slaves, we now call these people Afro-Surinamese. Susa is part of the plays performed in ancestral gatherings, feasts. Susa is indeed a fighting dance, a play for adult men. The men face each other on the music of the drums, accompanied by songs, one person has to imitate the steps of the other. When he has been tricked into making a wrong step, his place is taken by another. The songs often treat relations between men and women. It is a dance which is GREATLY enjoyed and applauded by the audience at the feast. It is not original Surinamese, it is one of the*

*slave plays that has its roots in Africa, but had its own development in our country, because at least the song texts are not in an African language, but in a Creole (Afro-Surinamese) language.*

*Susa is not danced daily, only at specific gatherings for the ancestors. From time to time it is performed for an audience on stage, but then out of context, and dramatized for the audience.*

African war dances, physical and martial arts were generally composed of stick fights, such as the *el matreg* of Algeria, the Egyptian *tahtib*, the *donga* of Ethiopia and the *musangwa* of South Africa; and wrestling and grappling competitions, some with headbutts, kicks and punches, such as the *laamb* and *beri* of Senegal, the *borey* practiced in the Gambia and Senegal; and a number of stick-fighting practices and death and mourning dances, wedding dances, harvest dance festivals, such as the Yam Festival seen in a watercolor that appears in Thomas Edward Bowdichand's *Mission from Cape Coast Castle to Ashantee, with a statistical account of that kingdom, and geographical notices of other parts of the interior of Africa*, originally published in London in 1819, then reprinted in 1873 and again in 1966. This last example can be.

More urban and contemporary dances were also developed in Africa, such as the *kalela* dance of Rhodesia, described by James Clyde Mitchell,[62] the variants *mganda* from Tanzania and *malipenga* from Malawi, both part of the *mbeni* dance, as described by T. O. Ranger.[63]

# The N'Golo or the Dance of the Zebras

There is no doubt that capoeira has African roots. However, evidence also leaves no doubt that capoeira is an original Brazilian martial art and cultural expression.

In this vein, I must agree with Bryan McCann in Junius P. Rodriguez's excellent *The Historical Encyclopedia of World Slavery*, when he says:

> *Capoeira is a dance, martial art, ritual, and game developed by colonial Brazil's African slaves. Many of its elements are clearly of African origins, and have analogs in other parts of Africa's diaspora, but nowhere else did a similar game grow into such a rich, complex, immediately recognizable cultural phenomenon. Capoeira is uniquely Brazilian.*[64]

On the other hand, apparently there is a contradiction on Sully Cally's part, when she explains the origin of *ladja*, the fighting game of Martinique:

> *The agia, dance contest. In many books, the spelling of AGIA is "LAGHIA, LADIA, LADJA," yet, among the Bantu which originate most ethnic groups inhabiting the French Antilles, the "AGIA" does exist and designate the action of "chopping up," a term used to encourage two wrestlers in Mina dialect. It is quite possible after this deduction, that the origin of the name AGIA is Congolese.*[65]

We have already seen that "Mina" was a generic name given in Brazil to slaves who were mostly speakers of the Gbe languages that came from the Portuguese fort of São Jorge da Mina, notedly peoples coming from the Bight of Benin, as well the Akan peoples (also historically related to the Adja) from Ghana. However, these "Mina" slaves were mostly imported by the Portuguese in the fifteenth and early sixteenth century[66] from other parts of Africa including Benin, the home of the Adja peoples.

In addition, in the seventeenth century, the Ewe (i.e., Adja-Yorùbá) slaves – who had migrated from Nigeria to a large area near Lake Volta, Ghana, a couple of centuries ago – were often embarked onto slaves ships from the ports of Keta and Anloga, home of the Adja-Yorùbá, near the Togo border. The Ewe slaves were also boarded onto ships in ports extending all the way from Lake Volta, near present-day Ada-Foah in Ghana, to Lagos, Nigeria, which were the main points of embarkation of the Bight of Benin. Therefore, when Sully Cally exemplifies the origin of *ladja* as a "Congolese" art based on a "dialect of the Mina" – who were most probably of Adja-Yorùbá descent – she is actually confirming the "non-Kongo-Angola" roots of the Martinican fighting-game, the closest "cousin" of capoeira.*

Furthermore, the word *agya* has an Akan meaning of "father," "mother," or "heritage," which could explain the "symbiosis" of these two historically related peoples, the Akan and the Adja. In other words, the Akan used the term "heritage" or "origin" (mother) to name a pre-colonial tradition that had been retained in their memories, a recollection of their cults, rites and customs expressed in "their" new world, while the Adja organized and performed the celebrations per se. This cultural and linguistic phenomenon also occurred in other areas, such as the Kimbundu origin of the term *kilombu (quilombo)* of the Imbangala from Angola for the famous Maroon settlement in the seventeenth century, which was led by Ganga Zumba – according to Robert Nelson Anderson III, a man who was probably a native of Palmares with a Bantu title and an Adja origin.

Much has already been said about this dance-fight in Angola that has "perhaps been the precursor of capoeira." Sources who defend this theory call it N'Golo, or the Dance of the Zebras. Some good authors have even written about it; others affirm its existence as a cultural legacy of Angola, and say that Angola is going to go back to its roots and "recover their forgotten capoeira." I wish it weren't needless to say that Angola has never even heard of such a dance-fight during the colonial times and it does not officially recognize it as a national sport or cultural expression.

---

*You can read more about the Mina slaves in Gwendolyn Midlo Hall's excellent *African ethnicities and the meanings of 'Mina'* in Paul E. Lovejoy and David Vincent Trotman's *Trans-Atlantic Dimensions of Ethnicity in the African Diaspora* (London, 2003) and in *Slavery and African Ethnicities in the Americas: Restoring the Links* (United States, 2005). Additionally, I recommend *Ethnicities of Enslaved Africans in the Diaspora: On the Meanings of "Mina" (Again)*, by Robin Law, in History of Africa, Volume 32 (United States, 2005).

Afro-descendants, especially those who are descendants of the Atlantic slave trade in the Americas, do not need to create a new bridge from their ancestry to Africa, nor Angola, in order to justify their black pride and their sense of African unification. This connection, along with its African dignity, is already there; it has always been there, connecting all African Americans in the broader geographic sense. And this includes Brazil, mainly, I would say, due to its importance in the Atlantic slave trade scenario, but mostly in terms of the Brazilian capoeira.

Each of the countries that took part in the slave trade has a rich and important African legacy to share with society in its own way and in its own right. Herskovits's book approaches the issue of cultural differences in the U.S. in what fits universally in the former enslaved Americas. From the foreword:

*There is an understandable tendency in our civilization to order our thoughts with reference to sequence in time and to think in terms of origins.*[67]

Capoeira is one beautiful example of the integration and inter-dependence of white and blacks in a way that it should be used as an unprecedented anthropological example for American societies. While the roots and the motive were born from African seeds in Brazil, the fascination and the recognition of its expression among the white population created a unique symbiosis that would otherwise be impossible given a different time-frame, or the social condition of blacks during the slave trade period, up to the mid-twentieth century.

Still in the late nineteenth century, the black population in Brazil was socially and economically alienated as a byproduct of slavery, which were only abolished in 1888, and where racism and economic disadvantage was also a visible legacy. In this scenario, cultural expressions generally tend to shrink with their actors, or to idle and agonize in history, as if Picasso painted for himself, leaving his paintings in his closet and never showed them in public.

The good news is that this did not happen in Brazil (nor to Picasso!), and although much needs to be done for the black population in Brazil, which has the largest population of black origin outside of Africa, the Afro-Brazilian cultural expressions were soon acknowledged by the white upper classes (i.e., the ones who held the power), first as a means of curiosity about the exotic and later as their own form of expression and amusement. Nowadays, Afro-Brazilian culture is a vital part of Brazilian national pride.

Due to the masses of slaves in the longest period of Atlantic slave trade in the history of the Americas (Brazil was the last country in the Western Hemisphere to abolish slavery), and because of this early integration, in which those of European descent and those of African descent comingled, black–white relations in Brazil started flourishing even during the slavery years. I am not saying here that there is no prejudice in Brazil. Some say there is racial prejudice while others swear there is only class prejudice. Most authors agree with Florestan Fernandes that Brazil is one of the most racially tolerant nations in the world.[68] Important here is the cultural miscegenation that worked for both sides of the story. Herskovits writes about the retention of Africanisms in America, where, for a number of reasons that differentiate the Brazilian and American slavery systems, the black people in the U.S. historically retained fewer Africanisms than the blacks in Brazil. Again from the book's foreword:

*[...] cultural differentials are so important in the social adjustment of different peoples to each other that the retention even of cultural fragments from Africa may introduce serious problems into Negro-white relations.*

*On the positive side, the origin of the distinctive cultural contributions of the Negro to American life must not be overlooked. Furthermore, and entirely apart from immediate practical considerations, the social scientist can learn about the general nature of cultural development from the cultural history of the Negro in America.*[69]

However, we are looking at two phenomena under the same category and historic period. The white dominant people in Brazil had more time and favorable conditions to benefit from the contributions of the Africanisms, whereas in the U.S., for instance, this cultural retention was less common. This cultural difference is not only because of the higher proportion of whites to blacks in the American South, or the absence of remote or inaccessible retreats where runaway slaves could have developed stable Maroon communities like the Brazilian *quilombos* with little or no white interference, but also due to this blending of cultures that interested both sides: the Europeans (and their descendants) and the Africans (and their descendants). As Edwin R. Embree explains:

> *Torn from their previous environment, Africans found themselves grouped in the homesteads and plantations of America with fellow blacks from divergent tribes whose customs differed widely, whose languages even they could not understand. A new life had to be formed and was formed in the pattern of the New World. The old African tribal society was completely destroyed. From membership in their primitive social units, Negroes were forced into the organization required by the plantation and by the demands of the particular American families to which they were attached. The only folkways that had elements in common for all the slaves were those they found about them in America. The Africans began to take hold of life where they could. They began to speak English, to take up the Christian religion, to fall into the labor pattern demanded by American needs and customs, to fit themselves as best they could into all the mores of the New World.*[70]

Herskovits leaves us with the clear notion that African cultural retentions in the U.S. were strong when, and where, conditions were more favorable, as was the case with the inhabitants of coastal South Carolina and Georgia because of their relative isolation at the time. With the more unfavorable environment of the American plantations and farms, slaves had no choice but to do what was necessary to survive in such a hostile atmosphere.

## The True Origins of N'Golo

Professor Thomas J. Larson describes, with fascination, various passages of the *Efendula* (also referred to as "Efundula") – the puberty and marriage festivities he watched while visiting the Bantu Kwanyama tribe in the Ovamboland, Namibia, during his University of California expedition to South Africa in 1947 and 1948. These Ovambo people inhabit northern Namibia and southern Angola.

> *I'd heard there was to be an Efendula dance at this kraal. The Efendula was a combination of puberty and marriage ceremony for the young girls.*[71]

> *Great crowds of people have arrived at the kraal to witness the Efendula dance.*[72]

This next passage is of special interest, as it depicts the dance of the men. Elements of this type of dance, such as imitation of animal behavior, has been seen in several cardinal points of Africa (see John Atkin's description of a dance in Sierra Leone on page 102). But here, our most relevant point is the fact that there is no bout between two opponents, no combat of the "one man against the other" type whatsoever – not even a mock combat. The men are dancing to exhibit themselves to the women:

> *This time the men, the hunters were the star performers. Many of the dances were of a ritual nature. Some were danced for fun and others had a spiritual or religious motive. Most of the dances depicted*

*the life and the hunting of wild animals. By dramatizing the hunt and the animals which were hunted the Bushmen believed that they could have good fortune and it would help them have a magical spell over the animals. Many of the animal dances which imitated frogs jumping, troops of monkeys and baboons frolicking, and snakes lying in wait at the water hole were imitated. The more serious dances of the men dramatized the hunt, the pursuit of men and their dogs after the ostrich, the kudu, the eland and many animals of the veld they commonly hunted. Many of the Bushmen rock paintings depict these dances.*[73]

There is no doubt that there are elements in Larson's descriptions of the *efundula* that could have been imported to capoeira, such as the *macaco*, the "jump of the monkey," which is an old traditional move in capoeira (see the list of capoeira moves and the phonological transcriptions on page 189). Then again, here he describes how athletic the dance that he saw was, and explains that the dance of the men was an acrobatic contest, meaning that each "contestant" tried to dance better than the other in a clear individual demonstration of skills:

*Never before had I seen such vigorous dancing. The gyrations of the American jive and jitterburg dancing were child's play in comparison with the movements of the men who danced to the complicated drum beats of a half-dozen long hollowed out logs covered at one end by rawhide.*

*The magical thumping rhythms of the drums, stirs one into instant desire to dance. All the men were dressed in European clothes minus the shoes, which was a great contrast to the barbaric movements of the dance. The dance of the men was an athletic and acrobatic contest. Each contestant tries to do his utmost to dance better than others. All the men were dressed in European clothes minus the shoes, which was a great contrast to the barbaric moves of the dance. There was no set pattern for the dance as each contestant who ventured into the ring made up his own dance. Some of them jumped high into the air kicking grotesquely, turning somersaults, and kicking out their legs in rhythm with the wild tempo of the dance. Others threw themselves onto the ground then leaped into the air swinging their arms while the spectators clapped and shouted in glee and excitement. No two dancers danced the same way. The hot sun burned down on the glistening sand of the kraal and upon the dark-skinned half-nude women spectators and sweating dancers. But the sun rather than sapping the strength of the performers seemed to give them added zest and vigor in their mad gyrations. One dancer at a time went into the dancing circle until all volunteers had exhausted themselves in the sand and rising dust.[74]*

Larson describes these fascinating passages as the beginning of the *efundula* festivities, leaving us with a clue of what may have inspired the term Dance of the Zebras when he writes about the girls' dance:

*The serious dancing now began, the Efendula of the girls and young women. In the springtime of each year the young girls of marriageable age from fifteen to sixteen go through a weeklong ceremony, which culminates into a combination puberty and marriage ordeal. Several weeks before the Efendula commences.*

*A half-dozen girls formed a line and each holding high a zebra tail fly whisk while they danced in unison advancing back and forth in rhythm with the pounding of the drums and clapping of hands of the spectators.[75]*

At one point, Larson also described the rhythm in the ring:

*... spectators and relatives clapped their hands and sang to the rhythm of the thumping drums.[76]*

There is plenty of evidence of the *efundula* in northern Namibia and southern Angola, with agile demonstrations of physical skills by the male dancers during their performances as part of the festivities. However, there is no evidence whatsoever of a bout taking place between two men in the *efundula* ring.

The term *efundula* means "kicking up the sand when dancing," and the "zebra tail" fly whisks of the girls may be replaced by cattle, or gnu tail wands when they are dancing. There is really nothing that suggests a "dance of zebras," "fighting zebras," or "zebra fighting styles." In fact, the zebra is not specifically important for the *efundula* dances. However, the terms *engolo*, *ongolo* or N'Golo may well be explained by the following passage:

> *Locally, the final hairdo before the girl went for her wedding [was] called iipando yuuwala wOngolo because of the mixed stripes that resembled the stripes of a zebra.*[77]

My suspicion for the origin of the name N'Golo leans first toward the phonetics which describe the final *iipando* hairdo of the bride. The word *"wOngolo,"* which is the last word in a three-word phrase, is clearly not pronounced on a slow, paused way, thus becoming more stressed to the ear of the European and American visitor. Secondly, my suspicions lean toward the word *N'Gola* by which the Kingdom of Angola was known. It would be very easy and practical for someone interested in the Angolan theory of capoeira to come up with the "tale of the N'Golo" in Brazil, taking advantage of the African phonetic and orthographic aspects of the word.

The impressive photographs of C.H.L. Hahn, or "Cocky Hahn," during the period of his service as Native Commissioner of Ovamboland from 1921 to 1946, include a special performance of the Kwanyama *efundula* ceremony of female initiation in Ovamboland. These photographs by no means suggest that a dance-fight was going on, but rather a demonstration of individual skills and traditions. Heike Becker synthesizes the description: "The efundula, obango, or olufuko ceremonies were thus the cornerstones of legitimizing female sexuality and reproduction,"[78] therefore, having nothing to do with a dance-fight, or a "war dance." In fact, evidence shows that, during the *Ongolo* (hence one of the possibilities for the corruption N'Golo), the men dance to attract the brides, as a means of proposal.

The Powell-Cotton sisters, Diana and Antoinette, inspired by their father, explorer and naturalist Major Powell-Cotton, also registered the *efundula* ceremony among the Kwanyama of southern Angola on film in 1937, which can be seen at the Powell-Cotton Museum in Quex Park, Kent, in the United Kingdom.

To my knowledge, and in agreement with Nestor Capoeira, Matthias Röhrig Assunção and several other international sources, there is no evidence of a dance-fight similar to capoeira in Angola, and I must add, in any part of Africa originally. Capoeira was developed in Brazil, as explains Nestor Capoeira:

> *Based upon what we have seen up to this point, I am going to propose the thesis that the fights, the dances, rhythms and musical instruments from different African ethnicities did not fuse to "escape prohibitions and to deceive the white lords" but, this synthesis happened after 1830 in accordance with a general tendency of the black community, in which, the armed fight, impossible to be won, was substituted by the conquering of space and territory through culture. And, that the jogo de capoeira did not have an exclusive center of dispersion, but sprouted spontaneously in different formats and in various locations materializing in Brazil between 1830 and 1930, a certain archetype existent within the black collective unconscious.*[79]

The N'Golo theorists maintain that, "still in Benguela, the dance developed into a foot-fighting style that was later used by slaves and outlaws as a defense and attack, and that this tradition continued in Brazil."

Some sources argue that "the N'Golo was used by the Africans and Afro-Brazilians as a form of spiritual and physical comfort as a response to the harsh conditions of slavery in the plantations."

Particularly, I find it very curious that most sources who advocate the N'Golo theory are African, or African-American authors and scholars.

It is perfectly possible that Bantu slaves from Kongo-Angola, including the Ovamboland region of present-day southern Angola and northern Namibia, haved brought elements of the *efundula* to the African and Afro-Brazilian slave and free communities of Brazil during the slavery period, which could have included the drum playing; the clapping and the ring, mainly as a form of fellowship and diversion; and, later, the *berimbau*, though I am inclined to believe that only the latter had indeed taken place.

# The Angolan Influence: Bantu Traits in Brazil

The relationship between the Portuguese traders and Angola began very early, in the fifteenth century, and lasted for almost five centuries. During the Atlantic slave trade, Portuguese was the dominant language in Angola, and many slaves spoke the language, especially from the late eighteenth century and the nineteenth century, when Portuguese was considered even more important than the native Bantu languages if one wanted to be considered as part of the new "European society" in Angola.

The African influence in the Portuguese language came first from the Yorùbá spoken by slaves from Nigeria and from the Adja-Ewe and Fon peoples embarked in the Bight of Benin, and involved primarily words connected with religion and cuisine. Later, however, the cultural proximity of the Portuguese with the "Angolanos" was eventually spread to the Brazilian colony and soon Angolan slaves working in urban areas contributed their share to the language spoken in Brazil, and several words from the Angolan Kimbundu

(Bantu) language were introduced, such as *marimbondo* (wasp), *quitanda* (small market), *bunda* (the buttocks), *caçula* (youngest child), *moleque* (street child) and *samba,* among others. As a large number of slaves in Brazil came from Angola for such a long period of time, it is not surprising that some aspects of culture in the two countries are so similar. Also, it is not surprising that this social phenomenon created a "cultural comfort zone," where it was easier for one to hold on to some kind of "known" heritage than to face a more complex, or "unknown" reality; language and cultural proximity played a crucial role in this case, as the "culture on a first-come basis" phenomenon of the Adja-Yorùbá peoples.

Historians are aware that, as early as in the seventeenth century, Kongo-Angola, Brazil and Portugal shared common interests and diplomatic relations that allowed for a constant cultural interchange between the two peoples, with slave-servants, noblemen and former slaves being able to travel back and forth between the Kongo-Angola region, Brazil and Portugal. Up to the mid-eighteenth century, Angolan slaves were supplied both by the Kongo-Angola region and by Portugal.

In this vein, the same practical reason that allowed a slave owner to name a slave João Bantu, Maria Crioula, or João Mina, also allowed for a generalized geographical description of a cultural manifestation. In the particular case of capoeira, the *berimbau* followed this path. Probably brought by Kongo-Angolan slaves to Brazil, or built in the Brazilian provinces where conditions were favorable, strong historical evidence shows that the instrument was not originally associated with capoeira or with any Afro martial art expression.

The *Huaiss Dictionary of the Portuguese Language* places the origin of the name *berimbau* as "probably" from the Kinbundo Bantu word *mbirim'bau.* However, we have seen several names used to identify the instrument. For instance, in Mozambique, we find the *xitende,* and in Angola it is called *hungu* or *mbolumbumba.* Europeans traveling in Brazil generalized its name, calling it *marimba, merimba* and *urucungo*, perhaps as an allusion to its origin in Congo. The *berimbau* was popular among Afro-Brazilian vendors and street musicians and was also known as *madimba* and *lungungu*.

The *efundula* festivities in which Thomas Larson participated in the Ovamboland of the Kwanyama in 1947 are clear evidence of the independent dimension of a Bantu cultural expression. In this vein, it seems clear that the *efundula* rituals do carry elements of capoeira (as do several other African dances), although not its form, which would only happen in the 1960s. Furthermore, it is strange that the movements of the Dance of the Zebras, or N'Golo, mimicked the movements of fighting zebras, as some authors insist, without any historical or practical evidence. In his expedition, Larson's report of the male dancers imitating several wild animals, jumping high into the air and turning somersaults in rhythm with the tempo of the dance, does not suggest zebras fighting whatsoever.

# The Berimbau Joins the Roda de Capoeira

As seen earlier, originally there was no background music in capoeira, except for the rhythm of the drums, which was used to mark the pace of the movements, or to dramatize the event.

## The Musical Bows

Pre-colonial musical instruments such as bows with gourd resonators were not exclusive to Angola, but were produced by distinct ethnic groups all over the African continent. For instance, the *kerewe* tribe of the island of Ukerewe, in Tanzania, East Africa, has a bow-gourd string musical instrument that resembles the Brazilian *berimbau;* and the Bása produce a basket rattle that is almost identical to the Brazilian *caxixi*.

These societies made drums, gourd rattles, harps, horns, guitars, banjos, lutes, marimbas, whistles, bells, gongs, flutes, trumpets, basket rattles, and even rudimentary pianos, using iron, ivory, bones, hide, copper, wood, bamboo, raffia, dried cocoons, turtle shells, stones, bronze, brass, coconuts and hundreds of other natural materials.

## Arts and Berimbau in Capoeira

One of the earliest drawings of the *berimbau* was made by the explorers Hermenegildo Capelo and Roberto Ivens, who drew the musical bow in *De Benguela às Terras de Iaca,* published in Lisbon, in 1881. The text, however, provides no specific comment about the instrument.

Several historical accounts leave no doubt about the presence of the *berimbau* in Brazil: Jean Baptist Debret through his *Joueur d'Uruncungo* (Player of Uruncungo), 1826, made it clear that the *berimbau* players were intended to draw the attention of customers to trade in the streets.

German painter Johann Moritz Rugendas left some beautiful registers of the Brazilian scenery, including the engravings from his watercolors *Jogar Capoëra ou danse de la guerre* (Play Capoeira or War Dance) produced in Rio de Janeiro, and *San Salvador,* produced in Bahia, both originally printed in 1835 in his work entitled *Voyage Pittoresque dans le Bresil* (A Picturesque Voyage in Brazil). Although I believe that in both cases the men were playing capoeira, there is no *berimbau* used in the scenes (see more comments on these images in The Arts of Capoeira in the Chapter The Rise of Capoeira).

Austrian-Bohemian scientist and explorer Johann Emanuel Pohl came to Brazil in 1817 for the marriage between the Emperor of Brazil, Pedro I, and the Archduchess Leopoldine of Austria, the daughter of Francis I, Emperor of Austria and also the Holy Roman Emperor, as Francis II. Pohl took part in the Austria–Brazil Expedition, which ran from 1817 to 1835.

In his *Reise im Innern von Brasilien* (Voyage to the Interior of Brazil; Vienna, 1832), Pohl leaves us not only a description of an instrument similar to the *berimbau*, but also an engraving showing what looks like the instrument in the hand of a vendor.

> *Blacks really like music. Their songs consist of the monotonous call of a chanter as the refrain, followed by the response of the whole chorus in an equally monotonous manner; or, when instrumental, of the sound of a wire stretched over a small bow, a simple instrument attached to a hollow gourd, which produces at most three tones...*[80]

French explorer and naturalist Auguste de Saint-Hilaire wrote one of the first mentions of the word *berimbau* and, surprisingly, tells us of its use by the native Botocudos before the African slaves reached Brazil:

> *The only amusements are dance and music of the Botocudos. They often sing but rarely play instruments. Those in use among them are small flutes made with pieces of bamboo, and a kind of birimbao which hardly differs from that of the blacks, but from whom they certainly have not borrowed, because they already knew it when Julião reached S. Miguel. Their songs are as barbaric as their manners. Nothing more than a group of words that have no relation between them.*[81]

It is not certain if the indigenous Botocudo have invented their version of the *berimbau*, but Saint-Hilaire refers to Second-Lieutenant Julião Fernandes Leão, commander of the 7th Military Division in Minas Gerais, who supposedly found the instrument among the indigenous people before they had contacted the black men. I find this possibility remote, as the indigenous Aimoré who inhabited the inlands of Bahia and Minas Gerais had known the Europeans for at least a couple of centuries, and were at war against the Brazilian-Portuguese military since 1808 in a conflict that lasted twenty years.

Curiously, Saint-Hilaire also mentions the word "capoeira" on several occasions; the word, which in the indigenous Tupi language means a forest glade, from *ko'pwera* (Huaiss Dictionary of the Portuguese language), is still disputed as the one which probably originated the name of the Brazilian martial art, where slaves and free men would find (or prepare) a suitable space to practice and play in the open forest or scrubland (see The Origins of the Word "Capoeira" on page 136):

> *I return to the details of my trip. Before reaching Mundo Novo, I already observed differences in the appearance of the landscapes: the most comprehensive change took place before my eyes when I left this house. I went first on a steep and high hill, whose side still revealed capoeiras...*[82]

> *This country was once covered [in] caatinga; but mainly up to fazenda S. Rita, I found these scrublands replaced almost everywhere by cotton plantations or by capoeira.*[83]

Henry Koster, son of an English businessman from Liverpool, born in Lisbon, Portugal, is considered one of the most important chroniclers of the Brazilian northeast. He arrived in Recife in 1809 and settled in Pernambuco, becoming a sugar planter. In his notes, he wrote that from time to time slaves asked permission to dance in front of their *senzalas* (the slave quarters) and enjoyed the sound of "rude objects." One of them was the conga drum. The other, "a big bow with a string and a half coconut strung in the middle or a small gourd tied to the bow." In his own words:

> *The slaves would also request to be permitted to dance; their musical instruments are extremely rude; one of them is a sort of drum, which is formed of a sheep skin, stretched over a piece of the hollowed trunk of a tree; and another is a large bow with one string, having half of a coco-nut shell or of a small gourd strung upon it. This is placed*

*against the abdomen, and the string is struck with the finger, or with*
*a small bit of wood.*[84]

Lieutenant Henry Chamberlain, officer of the British Royal Artillery, came to Brazil in 1819 accompanying his father, the Consul-General and Chargé d'Affaires in Rio de Janeiro from 1815 to 1829. A draughtsman and a painter, Chamberlain remained in Rio de Janeiro until 1820, a period during which he devoted himself to depicting picturesque aspects of everyday life in Rio. In 1822, he published in London *Views and Costumes of the City and Neighbourhood of Rio de Janeiro, Brazil (Vistas e Costumes da Cidade e Arredores do Rio de Janeiro, Brasil),* illustrated with 36 color engravings in aquatint, together with the respective descriptive captions. His watercolor *Quitandeiras da Lapa* (Greengrocers of Lapa), 1819–1820, shows a man playing the *berimbau* and is now part of the MASP collection in the arts museum of São Paulo, Brazil. (Several illustrations of Chamberlain's book were created by the Portuguese Joaquim Cândido Guillobel.)

In a similar drawing, Chamberlain brings us "Market Stall and Market Women," Rio de Janeiro, Brazil, 1819–1820, where the same man is seen playing what the author described as the *madimba* (or *marimba*) *lungungu.* This almost identical illustration was taken from the Brazilian (Portuguese) edition, *Vistas e Costumes de Cidade e Arredores do Rio de Janeiro em 1819–1820.* Chamberlain describes:

> *The Negro with a loaded basket on his head, though arrested in his*
> *progress by what is going on, does not however cease playing upon his*
> *favourite madimba lungungo, an African musical instrument in the*
> *shape of a bow, with a wire instead of a string. At the end where the*
> *bow is held is fixed an empty calabash or wooden bowl, which being*
> *placed against the naked stomach enables the performer to feel as*
> *well as to hear the music he is making. The manner of playing is very*
> *simple. The wire being well stretched, is gently struck, producing a*

*note, which is modulated by the fingers of the other hand pinching the wire in various places according to the fancy; its compass is very small, and the airs played upon it are few; they are generally accompanied by the performer with the voice, and consist of ditties of his native countries sung in his native language.*[85]

The Reverend Robert Walsh was an Irish clergyman, historian, writer and physician who served as chaplain at the British Embassy in Rio de Janeiro in 1828. His voyages in Brazil led to the publication of *Notices of Brazil in 1828 and 1829*. During a breakfast in Chapada do Mato, Minas Gerais, he could observe a black boy playing a *berimbau*:

*... there stood in the hall a poor black minstrel boy, who played a very simple instrument. It consisted of a single string stretched on a bamboo, bent into an arc, or bow. Half a cocoa-nut, with a loop at its apex, was laid on his breast on the concave side; the bow was thrust into this loop, while the minstrel struck it with a switch, moving his fingers up and down the wire at the same time. This produced three or four sweet notes, and was an accompaniment either to dancing or singing.*[86]

Walsh also describes two types of dance. One, which appears to be performed by a man and a woman, and another, which he describes as being of a different character, which he calls a "war dance":

*Sometimes it is of a different character, attended with jumping, shouting, and throwing their arms over each other's heads, and assuming the most fierce and stern aspects.*[87]

Reverend Walsh also observed the *berimbau* played in Rio de Janeiro accompanied by other chord instruments, which, he thought, were called by the general name of *marimba*, an *atabaque*, which seems to be perhaps the earliest reference to the *caxixi* played with a *berimbau*.

Another historical testimonial of the *berimbau* and the *caxixi* can be observed in the 1856 description of James Wetherell, who was British Vice-Consul of Bahia, and Vice-Consul of Paraiba, in nineteenth-century Brazil:

> *I think I have not named before one musical instrument of the blacks. It is a long stick made into a bow by a thin wire, half a gourd to serve as a sounding board is attached to this bow by a loop, which, pushed up or down, slackens or tightens the wire. The bow is held in the left hand, the open part of the gourd pressed upon the body. Between the finger and thumb of the right hand is held a small stick with which the wire is struck, producing a tinkling sound; on the other fingers is hung a kind of rattle made of basket-work, confined in which are some small stones which are made to rattle as the hand moves to strike the string. A very monotonous sound is produced, but, as usual, seems to be much appreciated by the negroes.*[88]

French journalist and politician Charles Ribeyrolles traveled to Brazil in 1858 and gave us this distinct description of capoeira, the *batuque* – associated with the *berimbau* – and the *lundu* dance:

> *Games and dances of the Negroes – Saturday evenings, after the last week's work and on the holidays, which offer break and rest the black slaves are allowed to have an hour or two for the dance. They meet at the terreiro, gather the others and the festivities begin. Here is the capoeira, a kind of pyrrhic dance of bold and warlike evolutions, under cadence of the Congo drums; there is the batuque, cold or lascivious positions that the sounds of the Urucungo viola accelerate or slow down; on another side, a crazy dance is performed, in which eyes, breasts and hips are in a provoking motion, a sort of an intoxicating convulsive frenzy, which is called lundu.*[89]

Many European artists depicted the capoeira during their missions in Brazil during the colonial period as well as in the early twentieth century (see Arts of Capoeira in the Chapter The Rise of Capoeira).

According to Edison Carneiro, it was only in the twentieth century, in Bahia, that the *berimbau* was incorporated into capoeira, used to mark the rhythm of the game for the practitioners, defining a fast or a slow game through the *toque* – the way the instrument is played in the *roda*.

## Ag'ya and Damyé: The Cousins of Capoeira

The relative aggressiveness of the players shown in Katherine Dunham's short films stays pretty much in the realm of their own rings, as it isn't possible, at least to a large extent, for these participants (or "competitors," indulgently speaking) to take part in any serious real combat, let alone to play the role of overseers of the planter's chattels due to their *"ladjia* skills" during the Caribbean slavery period, except, perhaps, in some individual cases. Furthermore, I remain skeptical regarding the adoption of *ag'ya* as a tool of slave resistance, as some authors insist but rather consider the art to have been used a form of escape for slaves and free men altogether on the French islands. In this case, the practice could occasion fierce combat between two opponents, once the game-competition was held within the limits of the event and by a previously accepted circle of people (i.e., the ring), whereas in an open rural or urban area, a real adversary would not be threatened by such a "fighter," especially if unarmed, as most authors suggest.

Dunham's description of *ag'ya* as "an acrobatic dance that much resembles the Dahomean thunder dance" takes me directly to a phonetic and etymological approach. Slaves in Martinique were taken by the French from Dahomey and were mostly from Adja speaking ethnic groups; the same occurred with the Portuguese, who took slaves from Dahomey in the Bight of Benin to Brazil. The *ag'ya* (also *ladjia, ladja,* or *l'ag'ya*) could have originated from early descriptions of the French (therefore *"le adja"* and the contraction *l'adja*) to name these contest-exhibitions based on their knowledge of the broad Adja-speaking peoples in the region.

The same must have occurred with the term *damyé* or *danmye*, also used to identify the *ag'ya,* and which could be a corruption of "Dahomey," meaning the principal ports from where the Adja peoples* embarked on the slave ships to Martinique. This is my personal suspicion, which I am backing with an etymological, phonetic and orthographic approach. I, however, was curious enough to ask Gwendolyn Midlo Hall if the French slave traders were aware of the Ajda ethnic group during the Atlantic slave trade in Dahomey (if they knew that they were bringing this particular ethnic group to the French Americas), and she kindly answered that "some French Atlantic slave traders probably could recognize the Arada/Aja. More slave owners in St. Domingue could recognize them."

## A Conversation with Vanoye Aikens

Something about Katherine Dunham's *ag'ya* films was really bothering me, and this is one of the advantages of having been a capoeira teacher myself. There is a compilation of her short takes from her visit in Martinique in 1937 and a clip from the Katherine Dunham Company from the play *L'Ag'ya,* taken in 1947. If you like capoeira or are a *capoeirista,* you will notice that in the latter video clip, one of the dancers executes an *aú* (the capoeira cartwheel move), which is never seen in the original 1937 movies.

I was curious about this particular move, thinking that the *aú* could be one bridge from capoeira to *ag'ya*, meaning that, originally, there was no such a move in *ag'ya,* and that Katherine Dunham had used the Brazilian capoeira

---

*In Brazil the Adja-Yorùbá peoples (Ewe, Fon and Yorùbá) were often referred to as the Jeje people.

that she saw while researching in Brazil and then used it to complement her *ag'ya* dance. Therefore, I decided to look for Vanoye Aikens, the original dancer who actually performs the dance in the video.

Finding Mr. Aikens was an adventure per se. It took me some time, but finally, on December 15, 2009, I got a Christmas gift from Patsy Garcia, office manager at Jacob's Pillow Dance Festival, who connected us.

I called Mr. Aikens that same day in his home in Los Angeles, and he was very nice, as I expected. He was getting ready for a trip to New York, but kindly answered my questions regarding the *L'Ag'ya* play. Most importantly, he did confirm my suspicions that the *ag'ya* performance in the play had elements of capoeira and other afrocultural expressions and that the *aú* (we called it "cartwheel" during our brief, but really nice conversation) move we see at the 18-second mark in the video was in fact an element of Brazilian capoeira that Katherine Dunham had added in the choreography.

## The Aja People

It is commonly accepted that there were two primary ethnic groups of slaves exported to Brazil: the "Sudanese" and the Bantu. However, this is a much too simplistic an approach and does not represent our ideal scope for the purpose of our analyses. For instance, Bahia imported more West African slaves (the "Sudanese") than Bantu, which represented the main imports of Pernambuco and later of Rio de Janeiro. On the other hand, slaves from Angola would often be shipped mixed with other ethnic groups from other West African ports. Slaves were also reshipped from Bahia to Rio de Janeiro and other parts of Brazil.

We know that these Gbe speaking people (Adja-Ewe, Adja-Fon) and the Yorùbá from Kétou, in the Dahomey Kingdom (called *Nagô* in Brazil together with the Yorùbá from Oyo, Egba, Ijebu and Ilesha), and the Mina, for instance, are all related to the Adja-speaking peoples of Benin, Togo, Nigeria and Ghana. We have seen from many different sources that early migrations relate these peoples with the Yorùbá of Nigeria, independently of political unity in Africa. People from these ethnic groups were brought to the Americas to work as slaves in the Caribbean and Brazilian plantations during the Atlantic slave trade, leaving an important mark on the cultures of these regions. In Brazil these Adja-Yorùbá slaves, including the Muslim peoples, were known as *Jeje*. These were peoples who had journeyed through present day Nigeria, the Republic of Benin, Togo and Ghana.

The relationship between the Yorùbá and the Adja peoples can be observed in their deities: All the major Yorùbá deities such as the Orishas (the Brazilian *Orixás*) and the cults of Shango *(Xangô)* and Esu *(Exú)* can also be found among the Ajda peoples (Adja-Fon and Adja-Ewe).

The exact origin of slaves taken to Brazil has always been in question due to the broad geographic regions from where slaves embarked in Africa, often from different ethnic groups that had been separated or for other reasons of generalization. For instance, in the 1820s and 1830s slaves from Bahia were sold in Rio de Janeiro[90] and many "Mina" slaves in Rio were actually from the Ashanti, Gbe, Hausa, Fante, Nupe, and, primarily, Adja-Yorùbá ethnicities – the *Nagô* who migrated from Bahia to Rio de Janeiro after the slave revolt known as *Revolta dos Malés* in 1835, calling themselves "Mina" to hide their Muslim provenance.[91]

The generalizations "Mina," "Bantu," "Guinean," "Sudanese" and "Angolan" became so common that it is very difficult to draw conclusions about the exact contribution of a specific ethnic group to a complex cultural expression such as capoeira. Walter Rodney writes:

*A glance in the Brazilian scene eposes some of the problems and pitfalls in dealing with the issue of slave provenance in a planter's framework. The terms used to describe Africans in contemporary sources and subsequent scholarship are frequently so general as to be meaningless as a basis for comparison, examples to this effect being "Guinean" or "Bantu" or "Sudanese." Owners in Brazil used the word "Mina" to embrace not only the Gold Coast but also the "Slave Coast" and the Bight of Biafra, though sometimes they added "Ardra" (Allada) to cover the Aja. The name "Angolas" is also extremely broad, covering a variety of ethnicities leaving Africa via Luanda or Benguela, and thereby extending over a great deal of West-Central Africa. Planters who were supposedly experts on African groups did not seem to realize that the area tapped for supplies of captives was not necessarily close to a particular port of exit.*

*Some planters took good care not to allow a preponderant number of slaves from any ethnic group to be assembled in a single capitania or province implicitly recognizing as the operative feature not innate "tribal" characteristics, but the socio-cultural context which could promote unity and rebellion.*

*Conversely, a relaxation of this policy of mixing seems to be one of the factors which permitted an upsurge of revolts among ethnic and religious groups in the first half of the nineteenth century in Bahia.*[92]

*From 1770 onwards, Yorùbá were carried in such numbers from Porto Novo and Badagry to Bahia that they were able to transfer intact much of their religion and social practices.*[93]

As we have seen, many sources point the Yorùbá, Nagô, Jeje, Adja, Ewe, Fon, Sudanese and Mina as different ethnic groups when considering that the Bantu was the largest group of Africans transported to Brazil as slaves, according to statistics which do not take into account the real Adja-Yorùbá provenance of the slaves in Brazil. Firstly, the "Bantu" belong to a very large language cluster that is not exclusive to Angola or Kongo-Angola; secondly, these former ethnic groups also belong to one large language cluster, the

Gbe languages or the Jeje, with at least the six first groups mentioned above being practically from the same "main" ethnic group (the Adja-Yorùbá) and the last two in its majority, which means that, perhaps, these eight groups altogether comprise the largest ethnic group in colonial Brazil.

On the non-preservation of Bantu cultures and the hegemony of the Adja-Yorùbá peoples in the French Caribbean, David Geggus explains:

*This pattern raises the old question about why the dominant African influence on Haitian culture seems to have been that of the Ewe-Fon people, or Gbe speakers, of the Bight of Benin, whose vocabulary and deities are most evident in the lexicon and pantheon of Haitian voodoo. Into the 1970s and beyond, some scholars assumed these "Arada" slaves must have predominated in the colonial slave trade, though by the 1960s the pioneering work of Gabriel Debien had made clear this was not the case. If the Yorùbá legacy in Cuba and northeast Brazil can be attributed to the salience of Yorùbá captives in the last stages of the slave trade to those regions, why did the "Congo" of St. Domingue not leave a stronger imprint on Haitian culture? Were the colonists of the eighteenth century wrong to associate what they called "vaudou" with "Arada" slaves and especially the west province of St. Domingue? Given that captives from the Bight of Benin made up barely one-fourth of the colony's imported slaves, though nearly one-half of the Africans taken to Martinique, one might have expected the latter island to have more association with voodoo.*

*Several factors may have impeded the preservation of Bantu traits in the French colonies. The age and sex ratios of the West Central Africans were less favorable to the preservation of native culture than those of peoples from the Bight of Benin (see Table I). The latter's numerical predominance early in St. Domingue's history, as Sidney Mintz and Richard Price argued, perhaps gave them a critical edge in determining the shape of creole culture. Table II shows their clear dominance in the French slave trade in the period 1701–1725, when sugar cultivation burgeoned in the colony. Finally, as Roger Bastide suggested, the association of Ewe-Fon and Yorùbá with powerful African states may have won them converts on the plantations, whereas the Bantu emphasis on ancestor worship rather than pantheons of deities may have been more easily disrupted by the slave trade.*[94]

However, despite the greater Adja-Yorùbá acculturation history mentioned earlier, Angola rituals and dances were most certainly present in the Brazilian scenario, as described by Professor James Sweet, of the Department of History at the University of Wisconsin-Madison, regarding one watercolor scene painted by the German cartographer and painter Zacharias Wagener, who served for more than 30 years as an employee of the Dutch Colonial Companies in Europe, America, Asia and Africa, and who, when in Brazil, worked under the Dutch governor, Count John Maurice of Nassau. Professor Sweet depicts the *calundu*, a Mbundu divination ceremony that involved spirit possession.

The Adja, or Aja, were a group of people native to southern Benin and Togo. According to tradition, they are a branch of the Yorùbá who migrated to southern Benin, from Oyo, Nigeria, to Kétou, and to Tado and Notsé in present-day Togo, between the twelfth and the thirteenth centuries.

In the early seventeenth century, three brothers fought for the kingdom of Ardra, dividing it amongst themselves and founding the cities of Allada, later the capital of Great Ardra, and Abomey, the capital of the Kingdom of Dahomey and Little Ardra, later named Porto Novo (New Port) by Portuguese traders (present-day capital of the Republic of Benin).

The Ajda living in Abomey blended with the local people, thus creating a new people known as the Fon, or the Dahomey ethnic group, later the Kingdom of Dahomey.

The Adja, the Fon and the Ewe – also a branch of the Adja – and the Yorùbá share a common set of cultural and religious beliefs and practices and their languages belong to the Kwa subgroup of the Niger-Congo language family, with "underlying similarities in vocabulary and structure."[95]

## The Blending of an Art

During the seventeenth century, the Adja-Fon settled in southwestern Nigeria and southern Benin and Togo, the Adja-Ewe in southeastern Ghana and southern Togo, with the Akan people living in the west and the Yorùbá in the east of what was known by the Europeans as "the Slave Coast." The Adja speak a language known as Adja-Gbe, or simply "Aja," but apparently it is more accepted that the Gbe represents the general cluster of several Niger-Congo languages, which includes the Ewe and the Fon. The "Mina dialects," spoken by slaves brought to Brazil, for instance, was also part of this cluster.

From our specific historical perspective, slaves from these Adja ethnic groups Adja-Fon, Adja-Ewe (generally called *Jejes* in Brazil) and Yorùbá (also known as *Nagôs*), all of which were generically regionalized as "Sudanese" slaves, along with the Bantu speaking peoples of the Kongo-Angola (who spoke, respectively, Kikongo and Kimbundu), and Mozambique, shaped the Brazilian cultural scenario: the cuisine, the syncretic religions, the language, the musical instruments and the dances being the major expressions that form the rich Afro-Brazilian culture.

British surgeon Alexander Falconbridge, who served on slave ships in the second half of the eighteenth century, describes the embarked slaves from Nigeria singing and dancing on the deck of the ship:

*Exercise being deemed necessary for the preservation of their health, they are sometimes obliged to dance, when the weather will permit their coming on deck. If they go about it reluctantly, or do not move with agility, they are flogged ... Their music, upon these occasions, consists of a drum, sometimes with only one head..., and when that is worn out, they do not scruple to make use of the bottom of one of the tubs before described. The poor wretches are frequently compelled to sing also, but when they do so, their songs are generally, as may naturally be expected, melancholy lamentations of their exile from their native country.[96]*

In this new ambiance, a rudimentary form of capoeira was first developed in Bahia from early African games, most probably the same taken to Martinique, by these peoples coming from the Bight of Benin (i.e., the "Sudanese," Mina and the slaves from the Kingdom of Dahomey) and partly from the Kingdom of Bonny (from where slaves would be caught hundreds of kilometers inland), whereas the *berimbau* must have arrived with the Bantu speaking peoples of Angola. This explains some controversies and historical references, such as the *ag'ya* of Martinique – where nearly 60 percent of the slaves came from the Bight of Benin, acquired from Dahomey – and the *berimbau* being played out of the capoeira context and accompanied by Angolan songs in the urban settings of Rio de Janeiro, Pernambuco and Minas Gerais, before joining the capoeira *roda* in Bahia only in the twentieth century.

The linguistic and cultural similarities of the Adja "Dahomeyan" slaves and the Yorùbá were accentuated during the slavery period in Brazil, mainly through a religious fusion which produced strong ties between the Yorùbá and the Dahomeyan slaves. However, according to professor I. Akinjogbin, this cultural contact was so strong that in the early seventeenth century Yorùbá was the *lingua franca* of the Adja peoples[97] in West Africa. Moreover, as we have seen earlier, the Yorùbá were probably the origin of the first Adja people who migrated from Kétou (also known as Ketu); according to Sappho Charney, the Adja almost certainly had the same roots as the Yorùbá of Kétou.[98]

Both the French and the Portuguese used the ports of Dahomey (such as Whydah and Jakin), and Nigeria (such as Epe and Badagry) to embark Adja and Yorùbá slaves to their Caribbean colony of Martinique and to Brazil, in addition to taking Mina (Gbe speakers) who were transported from a variety of ports in the Bight of Benin, ranging from Cape Coast to Little Popo (present-day Aného) in Togo.

One other point of confusion among historians is that these Yorùbá and Adja slaves embarked on the Bight of Benin were often called by the generalized name of "Yorùbá." Therefore, it is not uncommon to read that "the Yorùbá" had strong cultural influence in the New World and, among others, that "the Yorùbá" used their religious beliefs and practices as part of the "strategies of accommodation, transformation and resistance of the African peoples,"[99] whereas we now know that we are really referring to the larger Adja-Yorùbá constellation.

In another vein, the *creolization* was a sociolinguistic phenomenon that acted as a bridge to complete the existent communication gaps between the different ethnic groups and their descendants during the slavery period in the Americas, and played a very important role in establishing the roots of the future cultural scenario of the Caribbean and Brazilian Afro societies. If, on one hand, the majority of the black people are currently disadvantaged as a direct result of having been politically, economically and socially subjugated, at least until very recently, on the other hand, the creolization was a global phenomenon with regional and linguistic characteristics of their geographic and political environment. This explains the *ladja* and the *quimbois* in Martinique and the *candomblé* and capoeira in Brazil; the *santeria* and the *mani* in Cuba; the *kalinda,* or *Trinidad Stick-Fighting* in Trinidad; the *susa* in Dutch Guiana and the *maculelê* in Brazil.

## The Creolization of Adja-Yorùbá and Angola Terms

The syncretism of Yorùbá and Bantu (Nagô/Ketu and Angola), plus the creolization, found in Brazil and in the Caribbean islands contributes to the difficulty in placing the exact origin of certain cultural expressions. For instance, Maureen Warner-Lewis tells us that, after analyzing the interviews done in Trinidad, it is not clear if their stick-fighting practice called *kalinda* was in fact performed by the first generation of African slaves in the region, considering that it was probably *"a past-time from second and third generation descendants and others;"*[100] Yvonne Daniel tells us that she "experienced the syncretism of Angola and Nagô/Ketu with some frequency in Bahia, but did not observe Angola traditions per se."[101]

I have heard from a street vender in Rio de Janeiro, where I used to eat a wonderful *acarajé* (a "hot" Nigerian dish made from black-eyed peas) that she knew this delicious recipe because she was a "direct descendant of Angolan slaves."

If you try to read about *macumba, umbanda* and *kimbanda,* most likely you will find Yorùbá and Angolan origins for the same expressions, from different authors.

We have seen earlier from Robert Nelson Anderson III that the first "king" of the Quilombo dos Palmares was an Adja-Yorùbá descendant living in a settlement named after a Bantu language, with a religious title perhaps given by the Imbangala.

In another framework, we have seen earlier that the slaves in the United States suffered a different distribution process, one which did not allow the same level of creolization that existed in the Caribbean islands and in Brazil. This helps explain why African traditions were so preserved in the Caribbean region and in Brazil.

However, the African American people have built a solid African American conscience (although nowadays many appear to be seeking a more "African" identity), and are socially and economically more integrated into their American heterogeneous society, which was a *quid pro quo* for the non-creolized (or for the reduced level of creolization) effects of slavery in the United States.

There is no doubt that the area of Kongo-Angola was one of the major sources of African slaves to the Americas during the entire Atlantic slave trade, and that the Bantu and Angolan cultures came to Brazil to stay. However, the Portuguese were the first Europeans to arrive on the Slave Coast, a strip of coastal land running along present-day Togo, Benin and western Nigeria, from which, during in the early sixteenth century, slaves were being taken to the islands of São Tomé.

From the Cape Coast – where they built São Jorge da Mina – the Portuguese started to trade slaves for gold with the local kingdom as early as in the fifteenth century, and later engaged in the importation of "Mina" slaves to the Americas.

In the last quarter of the seventeenth century to the first quarter of the eighteenth century, for a period of about fifty years, the Bight of Benin – i.e., the Slave Coast, had become the largest source of slaves to the New World, including Brazil – brought mainly by Portuguese slavers, surpassing all other regions for a period of time. Roughly one-third of all slaves imported to Brazil were embarked from this coastal region (perhaps much more if we count all Gbe speakers and include the Mina cluster further north).

Despite the fact that the Adja-Fon-Ewe peoples, the Yorùbá and the Bantu-speaking peoples had had mutual, interactive migration and trade much before the transatlantic slave trade,[102] the Adja appear to have kept their strong cultural identity attachments, perhaps through intermarriage, trade and religious system, and obviously due to their mutually understandable language (the case with the Ewe/Fon and Yorùbá). In this broad cultural context, for instance, the *vodou* was created – the same that was later taken to Haiti and to Brazil, where it is known as *candomblé* (according to some sources, a Bantu name for an Adja-Yorùbá religious tradition), before it became a part of these countries' own rich cultural history.[103]

In Brazil, this syncretism was so important, and the integration so absolute (despite the valid arguments concerning racial problems in Brazilian society, which, however, could be better translated into the discussion of "class" rather than of "race"), that one cannot simply talk about the "influence" that African cultures had in Brazil without considering the impact that the new Brazilian society still being formed had over these Africans over the years. We learn from Belarmin C. Codo that the level of retention of Africanisms of the Afro-Brazilian society was in a way so important that Afro-Brazilians also had a "wealth of contributions to the African continent" and that one can observe its "distinct phases."[104]

Gerhard Kubik, professor of Cultural Anthropology at the University of Vienna and an expert on African cultures, sheds some more light and helps us better understand the comparison between the Brazilian and the American slave societies:

> *There are abundant historical data to suggest that African Americans on the Mississippi plantations had much less freedom than, for example, African Americans in Brazil in Rio de Janeiro, where they used to walk around in the city on Sundays playing Angolan type lamellophones and scrapers. In the rural areas even drums were tolerated, and by the 1820s, Afro Brazilian community spirit included what clearly was training for insurrection: I mean Capoeira. I have discussed the relevant sources in my book Angolan Traits in Black Music, Games and Dances of Brazil. This contrasted with the life in captivity on the farms of the so-called deep South, by which we understand the vast territory from central Georgia to East Texas and up the Mississippi River. An exception that was the culture of New Orleans in the early and mid-19th century as described by George Washington Cable and others. That was an urban mix, and there was drumming.*[105]

## The Origins of the Word "Capoeira"

*Capoeira: second growth of vegetation after land has been cleared.*
*Also applied to [a] kind of basket made of native grass; also to the*

*Brazilian equivalent to jiu-jit-su; genuine capoeira adepts have remarkable muscular control. The term capoeira is also applied to a certain dance.**

Antenor Nascente says that capoeira is related to the *uru (odontophorus capueira-spix)*, a bird species in which the male is very jealous and fights violently against his rival who dares to enter his realm, and the fight movements resemble those of capoeira. However, I find this very improbable, as *capueira-spix* was named by German naturalist Johann Baptist Ritter von Spix, member of the Bavarian Academy of Sciences, who first recorded the spot-winged wood-quail, called *uru,* in 1824–1825, in the publication entitled *Avium species novae.*

Gerhard Kubik also contributed to my Adja-Yorùbá theory:

*It is quite possible that Yorùbá concepts about the music background of wrestling games slipped into capoeira at a stage when it began to lose its older social context…*

*Traditions to accompany fighting games with musical instruments are not restricted at all to Angola and Southern Africa.*[106]

Professor Kubik adds that he finds it strange "that the Brazilians use the name capoeira de Angola, since there's no such an art-form in Angola."

However, although we should not accept it as final, we should consider one possibility raised by Kubik concerning the provenance of the term "capoeira": In the Bantu region of Angola, the word *ka/pwe/re* is a verb of the Umbundu language of the Ovimbundu, which means "clap."

*\*From Brazil – Today and Tomorrow, by L. E. Eliott (United States, 2007), pp. 325.*

In my opinion, Kubik's theory is a strong one; however, I'd stick to the Tupi Brazilian Indian word *ko'pwera*, meaning a forest glade,* "where slaves and free men would prepare or find a suitable space to practice and play in the open forest or scrubland."

A 1972 newspaper interview with mestre Bimba in the *Jornal do Brasil* suggested that he adopted the name of Capoeira Regional in response to a bureaucratic process that would not openly support its African heritage. When he went to the Education Secretary of Bahia to officially register the name "Capoeira de Angola," the term Angola was rejected. As a result, it was necessary for Bimba "to re-submit the term *luta regional* [regional fight] in order for it to be accepted."[107]

## Batuque Rituals, Nations and Candomblé

The religions and rites of African origin have been part of the Brazilian scenario since the sixteenth century, brought from Africa by black slaves, stripped of their land and sent to a new country, where they managed to worship their gods.

Not trying to exhaust the subject – but presenting additional consistent evidence of the Adja-Yorùbá contribution to the Brazilian African arts and culture – this section explores a little of the African religious expressions in Brazil in general and in Rio Grande do Sul specifically, where the Batuque rituals of *orishas* were fairly preserved.

### Batuque, the Cult of Orishas

The *batuque* cult of the *orishas* started in Rio Grande do Sul in the early nineteenth century.

---

*Houaiss Dicionário da Língua Portuguesa.*

Here is a great example of the complexity, richness and syncretism of the Adja-Yorùbá (and Angolan) religions and beliefs in Brazil. The "nations" and the mixing with the different ethnic and geographic regions of origin in Africa, the process of acculturation explained by David Geggus, justifies the reason why the Adja-Yorùbá took the lead in the most important cultural manifestations in the country (as well as in the Caribbean islands).

In the beginning, it was very difficult for the Adja-Yorùbá slaves to practice their rituals, so they used the saints of the Catholic religion in order to hide their African rites. Nowadays, this has disappeared in some *terreiros* (temples) of "African nations."

Many old *babalorixás* ("babalorishas," the leading male priest often called "father of saint") and *yalorixás* ("yalorishas," the leading female priest often called "mother of saint") refused to teach even to those who deserved to learn, afraid of misusing their religion. "It would be so nice if we could recover half of the wisdom of our ancestors," says Eduardo Cezimbra, the Babalorixá Tita de Xangô, from Rio Grande do Sul, south of Brazil.[108]

## The Ijexá Nation

These African religions, which used to belong exclusively to the natives of Africa, have spread almost to the entire world; today, the *orishas* draw the attention of anthropologists, scholars, researchers – some even siding with the heart of the African cultures. According to Cezimbra, "the African religion offers one of the most beautiful rituals of our planet, it is a so vast science that, when we grow old, die, we will never know all there is to be known from the religion."

One of the complexities of the Afro-religions is the way they adapted to their time, to the rural, urban (and of course spiritual) settings of their history.

There are different concepts about the cult of the *orishas* in Brazil; each nation and each region of the country has a way to deal with and worship the *orishas*.

Cezimbra's explanation, full of rich details, takes us directly to the points we have been discussing extensively in this book, which is how ethnic groups were perceived in the Americas, and in particular in Brazil, and how cultures were mixed (especially in the late nineteenth and early twenty centuries). According to Cezimbra, in the south of Brazil, for instance – which imported many Yorùbá as well as Angolan slaves from Bahia and from Rio de Janeiro during the slavery period in Brazil – there are, besides the Ijexá (Ijesha) nation, the Cabinda, Jeje and Oyo. These nations also use the Ijexá principles, as the latter is one of the best-preserved nations in the south – "especially because the prayers in Yorùbá serve the rituals of the nations."

Again, it is crucial to analyze the presence of original pre-colonial Yorùbá regions such as Ijesa and Oyo (from which Africans were initially disembarked as slaves in Bahia), associated with the Gbe language cluster of the Adja and with the Angolan region of Cabinda.

## The Cabinda Nation, an Adja-Yorùbá Tradition

The nation called Cabinda, originally from Angola, adopted the Yorùbá pantheon of *orishas*, although these Bantu deities are originally called *inquice* and *"clearly pay homage to Yorùbá patterns,"*[109] meaning this syncretism Adja-Yorùbá and Angola was perhaps already going on in ancient times in Africa.

The *inquices* (Nkisi) for the Bantus are the same as the *orishas* for the Yorùbá, and the same that the voduns are for the Jejes. According to Cezimbra, "they are not the same deity, each inquice, orisha or vodum has its own identity and their culture is completely different." He explains that the ritual language originated predominantly from the Kimbundu, and Kikongo Bantu languages that are very similar and are still used today. Presently, Kimbundu is the second national language in Angola; the Kikongo comes from the Congo, and is also spoken in Angola.

Despite the Angolan flavor, the worshippers of the Cabinda nation normally resort to the rituals of the Adja-Yorùbá, since the latter is currently the predominant ritual in Brazil, the difference being basically in regard to the respect given to the memory of ancestors and the place where rituals usually end: the cemetery!

The syncretism with Yorùbá does not stop here. The *orisha* Shango is considered the king of this nation, and owns the *eguns* (spirits) along with the *orishas* Oya (Iansã) and Xapanã. The cult of *eguns* is very strong among the worshippers, as is the symbiosis between the two religious systems, with the "sons" of Oshum, Yemanja and Obatala being able to go in and out of the cemeteries during their rituals.

One may call it syncretism or symbiosis, but the fact is that we are looking at sprits that are called under Adja-Yorùbá pantheons, by Cabinda worshippers, who, in their turn, ask the protection of Adja-Yorùbá deities in a Cabinda religious stronghold!

## The Jeje Nation

The pure Jeje nation ceased to exist long ago, most houses practiced the Ijexá (Nagô) rituals. At the Jeje ritual festivities, the prayers are not in the Yorùbá language but in the Adja-Fon (Gbe) language, and the people dance in pairs, facing one another, alternating places according to the rhythm of the drums.

The drums used for rituals are like the drums of the Ijexá nation, although in much smaller sizes and always in pairs, one played with two sticks and the other following the main ones played with only one stick.

What we call the Jeje nation is the African ritual which is formed by the Adja peoples who came from the region of Dahomey during the slave trade. These Adja-Gbe speakers arrived in Brazil, settled in the northeastern and southeastern regions, in the states of Maranhão, Pernambuco, Bahia and Rio de Janeiro.

## The Oyo Nation

Most African rituals practiced in Rio Grande do Sul came originally from the interior of Africa, mainly from Dahomey and Nigeria, where we find the cities of Ilesa, whose people are known as the nation Ijexá nation and Oyo, the land of Shango, the *oba* (king) of Oyo.

The Oyo nation is very similar to the Ijexá (Ilesa) nation, in the *batuque* ritual. However, this nation is more popular among practitioners in Rio Grande do Sul, where its rituals are still very alive.

According to oral traditions, some priests explain that the rituals of the Oyo nation state that the "calling" order of the *orishas* in the *terreiro* follow almost the same sequence as in the Ijexá nation: Bara, Ogun, Oya, Shango, Ibeji, Ode, Otim, Oba, Ossa, Xapanã, Oshum, Yemanjá and Obatala. Others say that the old houses of Oyo first played to the male *orishas,* and then to the *yabás* (the women) in the following order: Bara, Ogun, Ossa, Xapanã, Ode and Otim, Shango, Ibeji, Oba, Oya, Oshun, Yemanjá and Obatala.

The fact is that, even in Rio Grande do Sul, where these rites have been well preserved, there are several different versions of the same nation, each one following the customs of its original *terreiro*, many following the "pure" segment of the nation, while others merging with other nations, assimilating other practices in their rituals. It is the syncretism of the syncretism, which characterized the Adja–Yorùbá–Brazilian–Angola relationship throughout the history of the slave trade and the development of capoeira in Brazil.

## Candomblé: The First Adja-Yorùbá Cultural Contact

*Candomblé*, a syncretic religion like voodoo, *santeria* and *obeah*, is a segment of practices of religious traditions, rites and African beliefs, brought to Brazil by the Adja-Yorùbá peoples embarked mainly from Dahomey and Nigeria. It was most probably the very first cultural link between the Portuguse and the Brazilians with an African people.

With the end of slavery in 1888, *candomblé* has been greatly expanded and had thrived since then. Today, about three million Brazilians claim to be followers of some kind of – and often more than one – Afro-religion, but this number may be much higher, since many followers claim to be Catholics for fear of discrimination.

As we have seen earlier, in Brazil (and on some of the Caribbean islands), the enslaved Africans had the opportunity to live among their people as well as different ethnic groups, rather than be isolated for long periods of time. This helped them preserve their ethnic beliefs, initiation rites, songs, festivities, their native languages, and the cult of ancestors, among other traditions.

The *orishas* of Yorùbá mythology were created by a supreme God called Olorum (Olóòrun), or Olodumare (Olódùmaré), while the voduns of the Adja-Fon and Ewe mythology were created by Mahu and Lisa, and the Nkisi *(inquices)* of Bantu mythology were created by the supreme Zambi, God and creator.

## Candomblé of Ketu

Ketu (Ketou) is the name of an ancient kingdom in Africa, where the Yorùbá and Adja migrated from southwest Nigeria and Oyo. The king was named *Alaketu*. Ketu (or Quetu) is also another name for the people who came as slaves from this region to Brazil. In terms of cultural identity, we can call them Adja-Yorùbá.

Much of the more traditional *terreiros* of Bahia are said to have their origins in the Ketu people. The Ketu *candomblé* is the largest and most popular nation of *candomblé* in the world, and, unlike other nations, the language used in the ceremonies is Yorùbá (the *lingua franca* of the Adja peoples, according to I. Akinjogbin). Other differences between the candomblé of Ketu and the others lie in the beat of the drums, the colors and symbols of the *orishas*, and the songs.

The foundations are passed orally from *orisha* priests, the *babalorishas* and *yalorishas*. The most known rituals are Padê, sacrifice, offerings, the washing of beads, Ossé, Xirê, Olubajé, waters of Obatala, Ipeté of Oshun and Axexê. Another important difference between the candomblé of Ketu and the others is the relation to the cult of *eguns*: there is a priest prepared for this specific ritual called Oje, or Baba Oje, which makes use of an *ixãn* (a branch of a tree) to dominate the *eguns*, according to oral traditions.

## Candomblé of Angola

The candomblé de Angola is an Afro-Brazilian religion of Bantu origin, which comprises the nations of Angola and Congo, and was developed among African slaves who spoke the Kikongo and Kimbundu languages, and who are easily recognized by the different singing, dancing and beat of their drums.

In the hierarchy of the candomblé de Angola, the most important title of a man is the *tata nkisi,* and for a woman, *mametu nkisi*, which correspond to the *babalorisha* and *yalorisha* of the Adja-Yorùbá, and the supreme God Zambi (Nzambi) or Zambiapongo (Ndala Karitanga).

In a specific Brazilian syncretism, the *candomblé de Caboclo* is a version of this nation which worships the native ancestors (the term *caboclo* is used to describe a person of mixed Amerindian and European descent in Brazil).

The rituals of the Angola nation begin with the *massangá*, which is the baptism in the initiate's head, made with fresh water and *obi* (a seed of an African palm tree). There is the *bori* with sacrifice of animals for the use of blood *(menga);* the shaving ritual, known as the "making of a saint, the ritual of obligation of one year and the ritual of obligation of three years – which changes the degree of initiation; the ritual of abligation of five years, with the use of fruit; and the obligation of seven years, when the initiate receives his post, elevated to the degree of *Tata Nkisi* or *Mametu Nkisi* (both "caretakers"). After seven years of obligations, they must be renewed in order to preserve the strength of the individual so he or she can become a *Kukala ni nguzu*, which means "a strong being." Another old system of consultation is the *ngombo*, in which the guesser is called *kambuna*.

## Samba: Poetry in the Feet

*Porque o samba nasceu lá na Bahia*
*E se hoje ele é branco na poesia*
*Se hoje ele é branco na poesia*
*Ele é negro demais no coração*

*"Because the samba was born in Bahia, and if today it is white in the poetry, if today it is white in the poetry, it is very much black in the heart"* (my free translation). In this passage I don't dare try to translate again, Brazilian poet and composer Vinicius de Moraes makes clear where the *samba* was born. The *samba* is one of the most famous of the various forms of musical expressions originated from African roots in Brazil. According to most sources, the name *samba* most likely comes from the Angolan religious rhythm known as *mesemba*.

However, according to some sources, the *samba* is said to have developed primarily from the *batuko,* or *batuque,* and the *tabanka* dance forms, which originally came from the Cape Verde Islands – where African slaves embarked to Brazil – in addition to Spanish American and European elements. Floyd Merrell offers a more complete explanation, stating that the *samba* derived from *batuque* with influence from *lundu* and *maxixe* – which were also derived from *batuque* with influence from the Spanish *fandango*,[110] perhaps "mixed with a little of polka in the nineteenth century."[111]

Therefore, *samba* is indeed a Brazilian dance – probably born from original Adja-Yorùbá roots with a Mandinka and Congolese accent and European spice.

Johann Moritz Rugendas's watercolor entitled *Batuque* (1835), from his *Viagem Pitoresca Através do Brasil* (Picturesque Voyage to Brazil), depicts a Brazilian *batuque* scene, while Augustus Earle painted *Negro Fandango* (1822) in a public square of Rio de Janeiro, though the word "fandango" does not do justice to the painting, which in reality depicts a *lundu* scene. Both watercolor reproductions are part of the color pages included in this edition.

The rich cultural syncretism and symbiosis for which I have been arguing throughout this book can explain the simplification of "Bantu," "Congolese" or "Congo-Angolan" origins for most of what is African in Brazil, almost as an immediate resource to justify their origins. This phenomenon is also present in the Argentinian *tango,* which, according to Fernando Ortiz, comes from the Congo-African *iango* dance. On the other hand, Vicente Rossi, believes that the word is Arabic, though he explains that the sound of the word *tango* was given by the black community to their percussion instruments in Argentina, where "it was heard in La Plata from the melancholy days of the colony," adding that, in the colonial period, it was called "Tango of Negroes."[112]

Then, there is no doubt that the *lundu* has a Congo-Angolan provenance. What I argue here is that it is a result of a much earlier African experience, which ultimately was exported within African boundaries, as was the Adja-Yorùbá pantheons of deities, before being re-exported to the Americas, to Brazil in the specific case.

Malcolm Guthrie's classification of Bantu languages shows the geographic proximity of the Yorùbá in Nigeria and the Bantu in neighboring Cameroon, which corresponds to my suggestion of the inevitable historic ethnic affinity between these two peoples.

In a research paper published in 2009 by Genome Biology about African American genetic ancestry, Fouad Zakharia, from the Department of Genetics at the Stanford University School of Medicine, and a group of authors from equally prestigious institutions, conclude that, "There is a great genetic affinity between the Mandinka (Mande) of West Africa, the Yorùbá of Central West Africa and the Bantu speakers, who derive from Kenya and Southwestern Africa," adding that:

> The Bantu appear to have closest ancestry to the Yorùbá. This is consistent with the Nigerian origins of the Yorùbá and the presumed origins of the Bantu from the southwestern modern boundary of Nigeria and Cameroon, and the subsequent migration of the Bantu east and south.[113]

Peter Fryer, when explaining the African musical heritage in Brazil, reminds us of the first Spanish and Portuguese conquests of the Atlantic islands off the coast of Africa. In this vein, The "economic migration" Madeiras-Azores-Cannary-Cape Verde-São Tomé-Portugal and vice versa that I mentioned earlier, would not only be a responsible factor for triggering the Atlantic slave trade in the New World, "where the Portuguese would establish important advanced posts on their islands on their way to or from Africa and back to Portugal," but mainly to establish the cradle for one or more generations of slaves who had experienced different European settlers, "and were more 'educated' and 'acculturated' before being sent to Brazil and the West Indies."

Fryer explains:

> ... the black contribution to the emergence of Brazilian popular music continued and deepened a process of acculturation in the Iberian peninsula which had began in the eighth century with the arrival of Arab conquerors in Spain and Portugal, and of African slaves in

*Spain, and had been reinforced from 1441 onwards by the arrival of African slaves in Portugal.*[114]

Félix Monteiro, tracing the evolution of the term *tabanca*, relates it to the Brazilian *candomblé,* which, if he was correct and to a certain extent, throws away the purely "Guinean-related ethnicities" theory most contemporary sources advocate, forgetting the Adja-Yorùbá provenance of the Minas, the Adja-Ewe, the Adja-Fon and the Yorùbá who also came from this region, including the coast of Ghana, Togo, Benin and Nigeria. According to a number of sources, "Guinea," as it was historically used in an ample geographic sense, would be a general reference for the Atlantic islands closest slave ports, as well as a reference to the region comprising the entire Gulf of Guinea, including São Tomé Island.

In this framework, if the *samba* comes from the *batuque* and the *tabanca* of Cape Verde, and if we consider its Congolese origin, we should at least find a predominance of Bantu slaves living in that area during the colonial (and late pre-colonial) period of the Americas, especially during the time these cultural expressions were developed on the islands, which history does not record.

However, many Brazilian sources consider the *lundu* as the real origin of the *samba*, while others also relate the *lundu* to the *batuque (batuco)*. In this vein, as the *lundu* is probably a Congolese-Angolan syncretic expression originated from the *batuque* of Cape Verde, we should not rule out its Adja-Yorùbá provenance and later its extension to neighboring areas such as the Bantu (Zone A) areas of Cameroon before assuming its final Angola identity.

Writings of seventeenth-century explorer and Jesuit Alonso de Sandoval (1577–1652) do not make exactly clear whether the author is referring specifically to the São Tomé Island or to both São Tomé and the Cape Verde Islands. According to Sandoval, who researched the African ethnic groups from the Cape Verde Islands and Cape Verde* in Senegal to the Cape of Good Hope, including the islands of São Tomé, most slaves on these two islands came from the Slave Coast, from Allada, Great Popo and Tado, with some coming from Nigeria; these people were mostly Adja-Yorùbá and some Fula.[115] From the author's notes, apparently it is clear that São Tomé, one of the slave emporiums from where these Adja-Yorùbá traveled to the Americas in the early sixteenth century, shared an early cultural relationship with the Cape Verde Islands, and viceversa.

However, many (later) sources indicate that the early slaves in the Cape Verde Islands were from the Wolof, Fula, Mandinka, Balanta, Papel and Akan ethnic groups coming mainly from the Senegambia, Guinea Bissau and the Upper Guinea regions. Nevertheless, according to most sources, the Bantu – "the origin of all that is African in Brazil" – were not present on the islands during the early days of Portuguese and Spanish slavery.

The well-based theory of the Angolan *semba* and *lundu (umbigada)* can explain two possible phenomena. One is that these dances, as with the war and puberty dances we have seen earlier, could have sprouted spontaneously in quite similar formats and in different regions of Africa during pre-colonial times; or they were a "homage to Yorùbá patterns," i.e., a *cultural loan* from the Adja-Yorùbá people, which was later imported to Brazil, as Omari-Tunkara explains regarding the Cabinda nation that adopted the Yorùbá pantheon of *orishas* in their religious rites.

Dancing was one of the favorite sports of the African peoples all over Africa and, as seen earlier, it was not a privilege of the Kongo-Angola region. For instance, French explorer and diplomat Gaspard Théodore Mollien, who was one of the earliest European explorers of the West African interior, wrote about the dances he watched among the Wolof (Jolof) people of the Kingdom of Cayor during his travels in Senegal in 1817 and 1818, when on

---

*Guinea of Cape Verde, a region comprising a large territory from the Senegal River to the Kolente River (Great Scarcies) in Sierra Leone.

his expedition to discover the sources of the Sénégal, Gambia, and Niger rivers. His journey lasted until January 1819 and took him across Senegal, Guinea, and Portuguese Guinea. Mollien explains:

> *Dancing is their favourite passion; every thing is neglected for this amusement. No sooner does the griot sound, then every one is animated, and tries to follow the movements of the instrument by a thousand contortions made in cadence. The dancers keep time by clapping their hands. The spectators, to encourage them, throw their garments at their feet, as the most signal token of admiration. Lasciviousness presides over these sports. The ball commences with the night; the moon furnishes light, and day-break puts an end to it, and invites the musicians and dancers to repose.*[116]

About the origin of *samba* in Brazil, Mark Balla describes:

> *The origins of samba lie in a fusion between the indigenous lundu dance and the Batuque, a circular dance practiced by African slaves. By the late-nineteenth century, these styles adopted European characteristics to become mesemba and eventually modern samba. Spontaneus samba jam sessions called batucadas erupt in the streets on occasions of national celebration.*[117]

However, George Lang explains the early slave settlements on the island of Santiago, Cape Verde, the cradle of *batuque*, as early as the mid-fifteenth century to the mid-sixteenth century, holding that most slaves on the island were from Wolof, Fula and Mande, with which Alonso de Santiago appears not to agree:

> *The Creole genesis occurred at the end of the sixteenth century as a result of segregation of slaves from the Guinea Coast of Portuguese-speaking settlers in the southern island of Santiago. This process was called "ladinization" or training.*[118]

This apparent cultural, geographical and ethnic blend of *batuque*, *candomblé, Guinea, Wolof, Fula, Mande, Adja-Yorùbá (Mina) and Bantu* could perhaps be explained by the ample geographic sense of "Guinea" used by the Early European explorers, in addition to later contacts with the Bantu of Cameroon – despite not ruling out an early contact with the peoples of Upper Guinea and the Ashantee (Ashanti, a.k.a. Asante) people of Ghana.

Kubik explains the intensive cultural connection between Brazilians and the Adja-Yorùbá regions of Dahomey and of Nigeria, as well as between Portugal, Brazil and Angola. What Peter Fryer calls a "cultural triangle," as defined by Kubik, is also an important modifier factor, as history tends to repeat itself, but also it tends to adapt to the nearest evidence – as I see the "Bantu" provenance of all that is African in Brazil (including the unforgettable *acarajé* I mentioned earlier!):

> *The ships went back to Africa; there were African servants on board. Later, in the 19th century, wealthy Brazilian Africans traded a lot with cities in Dahomey and southwestern Nigeria. Afro-Brazilians resettled in the area and introduced the famous Brazilian architectural style to be seen in Lagos, Ibadan, Oshogbo and other cities of Nigeria.*

> *Ships between Angola and Portugal usually went via Brazil before Brazilian independence in 1822. In all, a situation emerged where in the periods of intensive contact with Africa it did not usually take a long time until a new dance, a new popular song or a new musical fashion coming up in Luanda or Lagos was known among the black population of Rio de Janeiro, Salvador or Recife.[119]*

When traveling in Minas Gerais, French explorer Saint Hilaire had the opportunity to watch the *batuque* on more than one occasion from different locations. He describes "Negroes of Mozambique" forming a circle to prepare for the dance in a text passage that may have helped contribute to the general assumption that the *batuque* was an original Bantu cultural expression, whereas several sources have shown Adja-Yorùbá provenance is more plausible:

> *The Creole Negroes were dancing the batuques while one of them played a kind of drum, and another, slipping quickly a piece of wood rounded on transverse notches of a big stick, produced at the same time a noise roughly similar to that of a rattle. In another corner of the court, the Negroes of Mozambique formed a circle in the middle of which sat two or three musicians who began beating in a rhythm on small little noisy drums. The dancers were accompanying them with their songs; and they jumped around in the same direction, and at every turn their movements were more animated. With bent knees, fists closed, forearms in a vertical position, each of them moved forward stamping their feet, and gave their limbs a sort of convulsive motion which must have been extremely tiring for the men who had worked throughout the whole day. But this violent state made them forget about themselves, which makes the happiness of the African race, and it was with deepest regret that they saw the moment arrive for their rest.[120]*

> *A troop of them, among whom were many men dressed as women, stopped at the place where I lived, and began to dance batuque; a fairly large number of women were to cross, and I noticed that none withdrew during this dance obscene.[121]*

On another occasion, in Bahia, where the *batuque* was first introduced by African saves arriving from the Bight of Benin, Saint Hilaire watched a performance of the *modinha*,* and apparently danced the *batuque* with a group of men and women:

---

*A sentimental love song perhaps of African-Portuguese origin, which was very popular in Brazil from the eighteenth century.

*Meanwhile, a guitar player [viola] sang the nose and throat of the modinhas, very silly and on a regrettable tone, to the accompaniment of his instrument. In general, as I have said, common people sing modinhas; the lyrics are far too gay, and through the air we could hear a lament. Soon, however, began the batuques, these obscene dances that the people of Brazil have borrowed from the Africans were first danced by men: almost all were white; they would not fetch water or wood as their slaves, and they did not believe that they were demeaning themselves by imitating the barbarous and absurd contortions of the latter. The Brazilians are very lenient about their slaves, with whom they so often mix, and who may have helped them with the farming skills they follow, with how to extract gold from the streams, and, moreover, were their dancing teachers... All night, we sang and we danced the batuques; the women finally got involved, and the next day when I left, they were still dancing.*[122]

# Samba de Roda: The Game of the Ring Samba

The original Bahian *samba de roda* was born in the Recôncavo Baiano. It is a variant of the *samba* that was brought to Rio de Janeiro and was performed in lower-class urban settings, in the *favelas* and *morros* (impoverished slums on the outskirts and hills surrounding the city). This vigorous dance is still performed the way it was created in Bahia, with a ring of people basically singing, clapping their hands and playing drums. A more complete orchestra may include acoustic guitar, *viola, cavaquinho*, tambourines, *reco-reco, agogô*, the musical triangle, in addition to improvised instruments such as plates, glasses, spoons and knives – all of these instruments or just a few sometimes with, the *berimbau* and the *caxixi*, especially when the event takes place in a capoeira school.

In the couples, dance, while inside the ring, a man or a woman makes a solo performance before inviting a partner to the center of the ring with an *umbigada* (the *batuque's* legacy of "belly bouncing," the ancient move of touching one's naval against someone else's). The couple then performs a rather flirtatious *samba* competition, a choreographic challenge, one trying to outdo the other with the best footwork and body movement, but never forgetting the sensuality of the dance's extremely rich body language. After a few minutes, the couple is replaced by other dancers who can also *buy* their turn in the circle (as it is done in capoeira). The dance is often performed by soloist women, each using the *umbigada* to call the next dancer, who then replaces her in the center of the circle.

## The Samba Duro, or the Pernada Carioca

On occasion, from the *samba de roda* the men engage in the *samba duro* (the hard *samba,* played in the circle). This is also known as *pernada carioca* (the traditional Rio's "leg blows") and *batucada,* a term that stems from the *batuque,* in which body contact such as cunning sweeps, trips and leg blows are often used by the dancers.*

## A Brief History of Samba de Roda

In the early twentieth century, in the center of Rio de Janeiro, the "Cidade Nova" (New City) is said to be the nest of the *samba de roda* in Rio. Freed black slaves, mostly immigrants from Bahia, joined the poor people from the northeast of Brazil who had come to Rio to find work. The *samba de roda* was a mix of *batuque, lundu* and capoeira, in which each participant would use his skills in order to belong to this unique environment, as long as it fit the

*The term *batucada* also means a *samba* music session, played only on the percussion instruments.

dance-competition, or exhibition. Eventually, the *samba de roda* moved up into the hills, where almost all early practitioners of the dance lived.

The Cidade Nova was the part of downtown Rio known for its boundaries with the North Zone and the poor outskirts of the city, as opposed to the south part of the *centro* (the city center), which shared borders with the rich and middle class. The neighborhood was also known for its rich urban popular festivities, which took place in the neighborhood of Estácio, at Praça Onze (Eleven Square) and at the nearby *escolas de samba* (the *samba* schools). Mostly, these events and celebrations took place out in the open, in front of *botecos,* or *botequims* – small, simple bars where people would gather to have drinks (normally the *cachaça,* the Brazilian distilled liquor), some appetizers, tobacco, cigarettes, candies,etc. – in public squares such as the Praça Onze, in people's houses and at the *morros,* which were mainly inhabited by former slaves and their descendants.

Soon, the rings of *samba de roda* would be joined by the white middle class and by Spanish, Italian and Jewish immigrants who helped build the rich *Carioca* (a native of the city of Rio de Janeiro) society. *Samba* rings would also be seen in the famous bohemian neighborhood of Lapa in downtown Rio, known as the cradle of the *malandragem,* the mischievous, cunningly quality of the *malandro* and the capoeira maltas (see the Malandragem and the Malandro da Lapa).

In 2008 the original Bahian *samba de roda* from the Recôncavo Baiano was included on the Representative List as part of the "Masterpieces of the Oral and Intangible Heritages of Humanity" by UNESCO.

## *Partido Alto*

Most *samba* sources believe that the *samba de partido alto* has its origins in the religious parties in rural communities where the *jongo* was played. The

*Enciclopédia de Música Brasileira* (Encyclopedia of Brazilian Music) describes de style known as *partido alto:*

> *Samba de partido-alto is a genre of samba the [that] emerged in the early twentieth century combining old (the partido alto da Bahia, for example) and modern forms of the samba-dance-batuque, from the improvised verses to the tendency of structuring it into a fixed form of song, and that it was originally cultivated only by the old connoisseurs of the distant secrets of the samba dance, which explains the name itself as partido-alto (meaning of a "high standard"). Initially characterized by long strophes or instances of six or more verses, supported by short refrains, the samba de partido-alto reemerged from the 1940s, cultivated by the residents of the "morros cariocas," but now not necessarily including the dance ring, and reduced to the individual improvisation, by its participants, of four-verse strophes sung in refrain intervals generally known by everyone.*[123]

## Samba de Terreiro and Samba Enredo

The *samba de terreiro* (also known as *samba de quadra*, meaning the samba performed at the courts of the samba schools) is a subgenre of samba which appeared around 1930 in the yards *(terreiros)* of the samba schools in Rio de Janeiro. The term *samba de terreiro* came from the clay yards where they were produced throughout the year, the spaces that would later become the *samba courts* after being cemented. The *samba de terreiro* was normally played by the *sambistas* (the *samba* performers) of the *samba* schools outside the carnival period, as opposed to the *samba enredo*.

Still in the 1930s, during carnival season, a *samba* school was supposed to present the *samba enredo* (the theme song) during the first part of the parade, and in the second part, the best verse composers could improvise with their *sambas de terreiro.*

In 2007, the IPHAN (Institute of Historical and Artistic Heritage) registered the matrices of the *samba* created in Rio de Janeiro – the *partido alto, samba de terreiro* and *samba enrredo* – officially recognizing these masterpieces as a cultural heritage of Brazil.

The Morro do Pavão e Pavãozinho in Rio de Janeiro was one of the cradles of a regular *samba de terreiro* meeting, which took place on the weekends at the Grupo Bantus de Capoeira. Several *capoeiristas,* from different schools and creeds would join Mestre Roque – the master of my own master, Adilson "Camisa Preta" (Black Shirt) – in this friendly environment.

I asked Mestre Gato, from the Senzala Group of Capoeira, about the participations of *capoeiristas* in the *samba de terreiro* during the 1960s, and here is what he said:

> *Right after the first capoeira contacts with Mestre Roque, we started to go to the samba rehearsals, which happened at Pavão e Pavãozinho. As we had a larger group of about 10 or 12 more experienced capoeiristas, the staff of the samba school invited Senzala to participate in the traditional Carnival Parades We would go to the rehearsals and the people at the samba school staff always welcomed us very warmly, even offering us a table with drinks. When we arrived on Friday nights, I remember that the crooner would say on the microphone: "a round of applause for the guys from Group Senzala!" and that was a party. We played capoeira to the sound of the samba rhythms and then stayed there later for fraternizing with the people, dating the girls, enjoying the night. It was samba de terreiro, samba de partido alto. This happened from 1968 until the mid-70s. After starting to participate in the events at Pavão, we also took part in the larger samba schools, such as Mangueira, Salgueiro, Unidos da Ilha do Governador, sometimes in more than one school in the same carnival, in capoeira wings, sometimes mixed with other groups.\**

*From a personal interview with Mestre Gato of Senzala, February 2010.

# The Jongo Dance: A Rural Diversion

The *jongo* is another dance that falls in the same category of Bantu provenance, probably linked to the cultures of West Africa with central ramifications in Nigeria and the Yorùbá people, before arriving in the Kongo-Angola region and to Mozambique.

*Jongo,* also known as *caxambu,* which was the name of the drum used in the dance, can be understood as another ludic blend of African cultural expressions, where music, singing, dancing, poetry and religion are expressed in the verses and refrain. Sometimes described as a "rural *samba,*" it is a legitimate expression of the African Diaspora culture in Brazilian lands, which started in the rural settings of the colonial states of Rio de Janeiro, São Paulo, Minas Gerais and Goiás, in the nineteenth century.

The *jongo* songs, called *pontos* (points), are related to the mysteries, traditions and memories of the black people, and are also played as a celebration of everyday life on the plantations. The songs are of a call type, pulled by a soloist and answered by the chorus. It is a community dance for men and women, where the participants form a ring with a soloist and a couple alternating dancing in the middle, producing movements that resemble the *umbigada,* or the *lundu,* which we have seen earlier.

## *The Ghanean Jongo*

There is a traditional *jongo* dance in northern Ghana, in the regions comprising Kasena (Kasana), Builsa, Bolgatanga, Sissala and Bawku, from where slaves were sent to European ships on the Gold Coast by the Ashanti and the Dagbamba people from Mamprusi. According to Salm and Falola, "the dance was performed in wedding celebrations, harvest festivals and funerals and was accompanied by different types of percussion instruments, such as the *kori* calabash drums, the *gullu* cylindrical drums, the *gungwe* hourglass-shaped drums, and by small calabash drums played with sticks, with *wui* flutes providing the melody."[124]

The main Afro-Brazilian characteristics found in the descriptions of the Kongo-Angola dances in Brazil are also found in Ghanaian dances, as Salm and Falola explain:

> As in many other Ghanaian dances, different instruments direct different aspects of the dance. Parts of the body adjust to specific drum rhythms, while gong patterns control body movements like spins and bows.

In Rio de Janeiro, the *jongo* was preserved in the neighborhood of Madureira, in the *favela* called Serrinha (hence the name *jongo da serrinha* by which it is known). It is registered at the IPHAN (Institute of Historic and Artistic Heritage) as a cultural heritage of Rio de Janeiro.

## Maculelê: The Afro-Brazilian Stick-Fighting Dance

The *maculelê* dance, like the *candomblé*, is a stick-dance originally brought to Brazil by the Adja-Yorùbá who came to Bahia, and, according to several sources, was most likely, further developed in Brazil to its current form from their African seeds under the syncretic process which gave us *candomblé* and capoeira itself.

In *maculelê,* performed in a ring of people accompanied by the rhythm of the drums and the singing in chorus, the sticks, called *grimas,* made of *biriba* wood, are used as musical instruments, meeting each other as the dancers' evolutions and coordinated gyros and *gingas* demand, always striking their own and each other's sticks together during the dance. The performers strive not to make any wrong move, or the sticks, made of hard wood, become an undesired weapon.

One of the most famous records available of the origins of *maculelê* consists of a funeral note published by the newspaper *O Popular* on December 10, 1873, in the city of Santo Amaro (also known as Santo Amaro da Purificação), in Bahia, which reads as follows:

*Died on the first day of December African Raimunda Quitéria, at the age of 110 years. Despite of her age, she still weeded and swept the churchyard of the Church of Purificação, for the maculelê festivities.*[125]

However, researcher Zilda Paim (Santo Amaro da Purificação, Bahia, August, 1919), a Brazilian educator, historian, folklorist, painter, forme member of the City Council of Santo Amaro and one of the most respected Brazilian authorities in *maculelê*, talks about a slave called Ti-Ajou,* who introduced the stick dance to Santo Amaro most likely between 1820 and 1850. About the origin of the name *maculelê*, she explains:

> *In Africa blacks fought holding two pieces of sticks, which they called Lelês. The rivalry was intense between Macuas and Males, the latter armed themselves with sticks and said, "Let's wait for Macuas with the Lelê." This perhaps originated the name MACULELÊ.***
>
> *The term "MACUAS A LELÊ" has suffered a corruption resulting in the word "maculelê." We know that the maculelê began in only two sugarcane mills: The Engenho de São Lourenço, property of the Viscount of São Lourenço, whose owner did not allow the Negroes to play with the sticks.*
>
> *The Engenho Partido, whose owner, Joaquim Pereira, agreed that the game was practiced in the slave quarters to disguise the fight and Ti-Ajou gave the music and the rhythm to maculelê.*
>
> *Let us hear this old woman, called Pupu, who lived for over a hundred years. She was a slave of the Engenho do Partido:*
>
> *"When I was little I saw there in Engenho do Partido Ti-Ajou, hitting the drums and playing the maculelê. When freedom came, I was already mother and grandmother of sun and grandson."*[126]

---

*Ti-Ajou is a typical Adja-Fon (Yorùbá) name from Benin. See DURAND, Guillaume (The Netherlands, 2001) in *Dialectical Anthropology: The Survival of Names of African Origin in Martinique After Emancipation*.
**The Macuas (Makuas), who helped inspire the term *maculelê*, were the Bantu-speaking people from Mozambique.

Pupu, the old former slave of a sugarcane mill in Bahia, explains that the slave Ti-Ajou had introduced music and dance to the old African stick-fighting practices to disguise the fight, leaving us with an invaluable documentation of the early, perhaps first, accounts of *maculelê:*

> *Very crafty, Ti-Ajou found a way to camouflage, and introduced music and dance. As a playful game and dance, it appealed even to the owner of the mill, who relented and agreed that maculelê was danced in the slave quarters in the off hours.*

> *Ti-Ajou was also a "father of temple" and, as such, he knew the candomblé rules and rituals. João Obá attended this group, as an eventual replacement of Ti-Ajou, as he was also "the son of the temple" and inherited all the burdens of the "Pai de Terreiro."[127]*

Regarding the name given to the sticks, Zilda Paim disagrees with the term *grimas* – perhaps an abbreviation of the word *esgrima* (the Portuguese word for fencing) – which was later coined by "Mestre Popó," the most famous master of *maculelê* in the twentieth century. She explains that the correct name of the sticks, *lelê*, means "a round wooden stick."

## Puxada de Rede: Poetry in the Fisherman's Net

There is a folkloric theatrical play based on a Brazilian fishermen's legend that is generally associated with capoeira and *maculelê* spectacles, called the *puxada de rede* (literally the "pulling in of the fisherman's net"). It is a poetic dance in which the men mimic the pulling of the net from the sea, telling the story of the simple life of Brazilian fishermen and the celebration of a successful catch.

Romario Itacaré explains the plot:

> *A fisherman goes out to fish at night on a jangada, a handmade sea-worthy sailing raft used by fishermen of north-eastern Brazil. His wife*

*has a presentiment of something wrong and tries to stop him from going fishing that night. He goes anyway, leaving his wife crying and his kids scared. His wife waits the whole night for him on the beach, and around 5:00 am, the usual arrival time, she sees the jangada. The fishermen have a very sad expression and some are even crying, but she does not see her husband. The fishermen tell her that her husband has fallen off the jangada by accident. As they start to withdraw the net, they find his body amongst the fish. His friends carry his body [in] their arms, in a traditional funeral ritual on the beach.*[128]

## Frevo: The Heated Rhythms of the Streets

### The Term "Frevo"

Modern accounts of the word *frevo* state that the term was born as a corruption of the Portuguese word *ferver,* meaning "to boil," which was mispronounced by the lower classes as *frever.* Both the music and the dance were created in Brazil in the late nineteenth and early twentieth centuries in Pernambuco, in the northeast of Brazil, with a mixture of marching bands and dances, including polka and some steps of capoeira, such as the *ginga.*

However, in the eighteenth-century accounts of Francisco Pacífico do Amaral, through his descriptions of the celebrations in honor of the State Governor, José César de Menezes, on March 19, 1775, the word *frevo* is found in this same context, in part of the lyrics that read: *Ferva meu padre a folia...,* meaning "Let the revelry boil... ."[129]

### The Frevo Dance

The dance originated in the old carnival street parades and festivities, when groups of *capoeiristas* danced in front of the marching crowds, protecting the musicians, dancing to the rhythm of the music, which eventually created the famous *passos* (steps), the characteristic foot movements of the dance.

There are some variations of the frevo, such as the *frevo de rua*, the street frevo, which is actually the original *frevo* with the band playing instrumental music, without singing; the *frevo-canção*, the frevo accompanied by songs to played in the carnival balls of Pernambuco, and also sung along the parades; and the *frevo-de-bloco*, which are the individual groups of bands (called *bloco*, meaning a "block of people"), which march along the streets, sometimes meeting other groups, culminating in a carnival frenzy.

Nevertheless, sometimes these meetings were not always friendly and fights between the *capoeiristas* from different *blocos* were inevitable. These fights normally resulted in many wounded people, and occasionally death, as many *capoeiristas* would bring hidden knifes to these exhibitions, which eventually would attract the police, who started to pursue the *capoeiristas*, arresting them during their public exhibitions.

As a way to disguise the use of knifes and other weapons, in addition to capoeira skills, the *capoeiristas* started carrying umbrellas to hide capoeira movements, adapting them to movements of dance.

The frevo can be seen every year in Pernambuco, during Carnival, which is always held forty days before Easter in Brazil.

## The Malandragem and the Malandro da Lapa

The famous *malandragem do brasileiro*, the Brazilian *malandragem,* has many interpretations today. At its origin, however, it translated as the "natural" *ginga* of the *malandro* (and not specifically the *ginga* of capoeira), a cunning and loose, easy-going way of being. In Brazil, people used to identify the *malandro* by its *jogo de cintura,* the "waist-game" of a people who were supposed to defend themselves against the hardships of everyday life. The main difference here between the *malandro,* an urban trickster by nature, and a common person was their interpretation of the "hardships of life," which, for the *malandro,* always meant very little sacrifice with great (personal) social or material gains.

As João Gabriel L. C. Teixeira, of the University of Sussex in the U.K., explains:

> *The genesis of the Brazilian popular music happened in this same place of oscillations between order and disorder, in the artfulness and malice of the "malandragem" of the end of the Brazilian Empire.*[130]

Adding that the malandro is a bohemian, Teixeira concludes:

> *For instance, it is said that every malandro is a bohemian but not all bohemians are malandros. That is so because the bohemian frequently professes an instrumental view of work as a necessary evil to make money necessary to provide for his bohemian life and the expenses that it involves.*

The bohemian *Bairro da Lapa* became the "center of excellence" for the *real malandro carioca,* and was also known for its gangs of *arruaceiros,* or *baderneiros* (Rio's own version of the hooligans), called *maltas.*

## Madame Satã: The Most Famous Malandro da Lapa

I met Madame Satã in the summer of 1974 on Ilha Grande, in Rio de Janeiro, and so did some of my capoeira colleagues around that time. Ilha Grande (Great Island) is an island off the coast of Angra dos Reis, south of Rio.

I was on vacation with relatives, I believe at a nice little hotel called Pousada do Porto do Abraão (something like Port of Abraham Inn). In my first day at the hotel, I was at this simple breakfast restaurant early in the morning, watching the last drops of the heavy rain that had pounded Ilha

Grande on that not-so-beautiful summer afternoon that I had arrived. The next morning, there was this man, I believe the owner of the *pousada*, and he was talking to me while I had my traditional *café com leite e pão com manteiga* (a cup of coffee with milk and fresh-made bread with butter). Perhaps he was little worried about so much rain for a summer retreat, or maybe he wanted to give me some advice for my first full day on Ilha Grande, since I had arrived the day before during the wet afternoon on a boat from Angra dos Reis.

Suddenly, this lean but well-built old (at least from the point of view of a 20-year-old *capoeirista*) black man, with short white hair, walking his little dog (if I recall, it was a white poodle) on a leash, passed in front of the hotel, walking as if he were Giselle Bündchen, if you know what I mean. He greatly piqued my curiosity, and I asked the owner of the hotel:

*"Who's that? A man that age, walking like that! He looks like a model on a runway!"*

And the man in the restaurant answered:

*"Don't you know who he is? He is the most famous man of Ilha Grande!"*

I replied:

*"Really? Who?"*

And, to my total surprise and excitement, he completed:

*"That's Madame Satã!"*

Next thing I knew, I was running like crazy to try to talk to Madame Satã, one of the most famous legends of the early twentieth-century bohemian (and criminal) life in Rio de Janeiro, the symbol of the *malandragem*.

Two minutes later I asked:

*"Sir, are you really Madame Satã?"*

*"Yes, yes… calm down, son. I am not going anywhere! In fact, I have been here for over 30 years and I don't intend to leave now. Take it easy, son…"*

And there I was, talking to a legend, as if he were a prize I didn't deserve.

Of course I was not even dreaming about writing a book about capoeira at that time; in fact, I wasn't even thinking about capoeira at all on this day, let alone about meeting Madame Satã. All I wanted that day was for the sun to come back to the island so I could find my relatives and I a nice beach to lie down on and catch some invigorating sun rays, and perhaps ride a canoe by myself (which I eventually ended up doing the next day).

However, there were a few important questions that I asked Madame Satã, which will help explain how easy myths are constructed from legends (such as the one about Zumbi and Ganga Zumba and the creation of capoeira in Angola) and, as Carl Gustav Jung said, "out of images, some false and others true."

The first question was if it was true that he has been in jail for "all his life" as I had heard.

*"For almost 30 years,"* he said, with a soft, nice smile on his face, the kind an uncle might wear.

*"Then what are you still doing here on Ilha Grande?"* I asked.

*"I have been here a great part of my life. I made friends here, don't have any friends in Rio… and I wonder if I still have some enemies there…"*

He said, lowering his soft voice even more, as if reflecting about the second statement.

Then I asked him if it was true that he had beaten and killed all those people, especially about the stories that he used to fight barehanded or with a razor against a troop of "half a dozen policemen" in the neighborhood of Lapa, the reason why he became famous in the first place.

Again, soft and kind – but now with a mischievous smile – Madame Satã answered:

*"My son, if five percent of what they say I did is true, you can count much more than that!"*

*"You mean more policemen at the same time, or more situations in which you actually engaged in fights against policemen?"* I tried to clarify.

*"Both," he said, now laughing.*

*"So what do you do here with your life?"* I wanted to know.

*"I am a cook! I even cook for some of my old guards at the prison on the other side. I am happy here, my son."*

Next I asked him one question about capoeira whose answer was really not a big surprise to me. I wanted to know if he was a *capoeirista*, a master of capoeira, like the myth (and the films about him) explore so frequently, perhaps to give the myth a "more Brazilian and mysterious" identity, which was really not necessary because he was indeed a very traditional Lapa personality.

*"No, my son, I never practiced, but I knew how to 'distribute some kicks,' and I defended myself with what I had in hand, and what I had in my mind, plus, people were really afraid of me, which was something that helped me a lot too, something that gave me even more courage when I needed to defend myself against bad people who wanted to harm me."*

Unfortunately, I don't remember other relevant questions that I may have asked this nice, delicate and soft-spoken person, who did not hide his homosexuality. I was (and am) very pleased with his kind attention to this then very young and curious *capoeirista* and future author.

Madame Satã died less than two years after this conversation and he was buried on Ilha Grande, according to his wishes. I went back to the island with my future wife to visit his tomb and pay my respects. Later I heard that the family had transferred his remains to Rio, but he is now back on Ilha Grande for his deserved, and now historic, rest.

Thanks forever for that day, Satã!

## Brief History of Madame Satã

Lapa had much fame for representing the bohemian life of Rio de Janeiro at that time – the *samba*, the cabaret life, the bars, the drugs, the prostitution, crimes and the police repression – all these things became a signature of this now historic neighborhood. With time, capoeira and the *maltas* were also associated with Lapa. However, Lapa was also a wonderful place to live, for families, children and artists, something that most people of Rio de Janeiro still do not know.

In the early twentieth century, a black man, João Francisco dos Santos, a son of slaves from Pernambuco in the northeast of Brazil, became its most famous resident. This young, poor, illiterate and openly gay genuine *malandro* in Lapa, *bom de briga* (good in fighting), as they say, was Madame Satã.

João Francisco dos Santos (1900–1976), the legendary Madame Satã (Madam Satan), came to Rio de Janeiro in 1907, at nine years of age, to live on Rua Moraes do Vale, one of the main streets of Lapa. He leaned to be a gangster from Sete Coroas, the biggest one in the neighborhood up to the day he died and left Satã as his replacement.

Satã received his nickname from a thematic Carnival Ball costume he wore in 1938 entitled "Madam Satan," with which he won the ball's competition. Satã was an assumed homosexual who worked as a cook for most of his life but never admitted being with another man. In fact, he married a woman when he was 33 and would spend almost 28 years in jail at Ilha Grande, a prison that became a summer resort island.

In 1971 he gave a now historic interview in Rio, to the famous weekly tabloid *O Pasquim*, the 1960s symbol of a rebellious generation, a politically marginalized paper that was above all a serious publication, despite its humor. The interview appeared in the book *A Arte da Entrevista*, first published in 1996 and again in 2004. Madame Satã always told this story and one of the many others like it, about how he was treated unfairly by the police, who ultimately helped transform him into a myth. In response to a question about the origin of his reputation for extraordinary masculinity, most probably in regard to the many fights in which he had been involved, he said:

> *I started in 1928. They shot a policeman on the corner of the street with Boulevard Mem de Sá and killed him, you know. I was in the botequinzinho and they said it was me. Then I was arrested. I was 28. Then I went to prison and was sentenced to 26 years in the House of Correction.*[131]

Madame Satã added that his imprisonment was "an injustice."

In response to the following questions about the shot that killed the policeman being fired from a gun in his possession at the time of the crime, Satã said:

> *The gun fired in my hand accidentally. The bullet didn't kill him, the bullet made the hole. God was the one who killed him.*

To me, after more than 27 years in jail, 29 cases with 19 acquittals and 10 convictions, three murders and about three thousand (mostly urban) fights, Madame Satã was a survivor. Indeed he was the last of the original *malandros* from Lapa and the Carioca scene, who did not know how to read or write, who never had the same opportunities as other kids, and who lived the life that was presented to him when he was nine years old and found himself in a prematurely adult environment.

## The Maltas, in General

The maltas are almost always referred to as *maltas de capoeiras,* but this is not the most correct term, as *maltas* could have members who were *capoeiristas,* also known as *capoeiras* (which in most cases was true), but they could also be formed by urban tricksters and hooligans who had nothing to do with the fighting game of capoeira, with their only intention being disorder based on their notion of society and urban expression. In some cases, for instance, there were combats between two or more *maltas,* sometimes between a *malta de capoeiras* and a *malta* of *baderneiros,* who did not have a single *capoeirista* among their members. Capoeira, knives, razors, clubs and stones were part of the *malta's* arsenal.

Members of *maltas,* who were seen striding along the streets, were immediately labeled as *capoeiras.* As usual, this association was rooted in the urban cultures so romanticized in the late nineteenth and early twenties centuries, when street fights, disorder and crimes in Rio de Janeiro were invariably connected to the Brazilian fighting game. But this is only a partial truth, as capoeira was mainly used as a way of escape, a ludic activity that was scattered around the city, first in the *favelas* and poor areas, and later in the middle and upper class neighborhoods, in organized schools of capoeira.

## *The Real Maltas de Capoeira*

There were, of course, the real *maltas de capoeira,* which were also known simply as *maltas,* and these groups deserve some elaboration.

These organized capoeira groups were born in the late nineteenth and early twentieth centuries and had specific functions, such as rendering services to local politicians or whoever contracted their services, which invariably included some kind of street disorder and disturbance of the peace at balls and public gatherings for– or as the result of – a specific purpose.

There were also those who would engage in such public disorders to provoke fear, get attention and establish some kind of urban power over the local society and the other *maltas.*

# THE RISE OF CAPOEIRA

I like to classify the history of capoeira in five main, comprehensive categories The first is the heritage itself: the African slaves and ethnic groups who were first taken to Europe in the fifteenth century and later, in the early sixteenth century, brought to the colonial Americas, influencing their cultures forever. In our context, this includes the most predominant players, the Bantu (Kongo-Angola) and Adja-Yorùbá peoples – who have left us a legacy of sycretized cultures with ancient African roots, which, as we have seen could be identified as early as the seventeenth century by Europeans traveling in Africa. Since practices such as the Adja-Yorùbá *candomblé* were seen in Bahia in the early sixteenth century, we could probably find here the "first generation" of *capoeiristas*, around two centuries before the term "capoeira" was used to identify the fighting-game.

Illustration by KALIXTO, O Calço ou a Rasteira (Rio de Janeiro, 1906).

The second is the very birth of capoeira in Brazil, still as a rudimentary fighting-game and cultural expression, with perhaps half a dozen characteristic "non-scientific" moves, the "second generation" of *capoeiristas* who were identified by Europeans traveling in Brazil in the early nineteenth century. However, there are two official mentions of capoeira in records of Rio de Janeiro in the eighteenth century, the most recent one appearing appeared in 1789, in a document that mentions the practice of capoeira dated April 25, 1789, with the fight mentioned as a criminal practice. This document, a record of the arrest of a black slave called Adão (Adam) who had been accused of being a "capoeira," was found by Brazilian architect and historian Nireu Cavalcante during his research in the National Archives of Rio de Janerio.[132]

However, Elísio de Araújo, in Gilberto Freyre's *Sobrados e Mucambos* (1951), tells us of a certain "Lieutenant João Moreira," who was already an expert in capoeira in 1770:

> *He was still an orthodox capoeirista – like those who did not have use, while in combat, of razor or knife, but of the head, feet and hands. Of those, it seems that the biggest one, still in the eighteenth century – in the days of the Marquis of Lavradio – was army Lieutenant João Moreira, by nickname, "the rebel," who, playing perfectly with the sword, knife and the stick, he preferred to use head butts and kicks.*[133]

The third category – or the third generation of *capoeiristas* – is that of "the old founders of capoeira," those *mestres* and practitioners who brought capoeira to the urban areas and started teaching the art in an organized way and showing it in exhibitions – both in an amateur and a professional capacity.

The fourth category is actually the most important, for it gave birth to the fourth generation of *capoeiristas* and the beautiful capoeira we all know today. This transition could not have occurred without adapting and transforming the art into a social phenomenon, an entertainment that became a strategy of social inclusion for some, a martial art for most and a cultural expression for all. Here we find the generation of *capoeiristas* who introduced capoeira first to the United States and Europe, then took the art to over 150 countries and counting.

The fifth and last category is the so-called "Capoeira Contemporânea," i.e., the direct result of the mostly still active fourth generation of *mestres* and practitioners. The fifth generation of *capoeiristas,* the ones that have the responsibility to carry capoeira into the future – to preserve its traditions while preparing the next generations.

# The Arts of Capoeira

Several written and visual historical accounts leave no doubt about the presence of the *berimbau* in Brazil. We saw earlier that in *Voyage pittoresque et historique au Brésil*, French painter Jean Baptist Debret's engraving *Joueur d'Uruncungo* depicted a man playing the *berimbau* to draw the attention of potential customers in the streets.

## *Danse de la Guerre and San Salvador*

German painter Johann Moritz Rugendas also registered a capoeira fight in the streets of Rio in his famous illustration *Jogar Capoëra ou danse de la guerre,* and in Bahia, in *San Salvador,* in his work entitled *Voyage Pittoresque dans le Bresil* (A Picturesque Voyage in Brazil), which can be found in its original French and German black and white editions and, more recently, in a Brazilian edition in color, from the original drawings which were both printed in 1835.

Comparing the two drawings, we can see a certain coincidence of movements. For instance, in *Jogar Capoëra*, Rugendas shows a man wearing a hat with his arms open, as if he was dancing to the rhythm of the drum, while the man next to him, on his right, seems to be clapping his hands at the same time the two men in the center play capoeira.

In *San Salvador,*\* we also see a man wearing the same kind of hat in a similar movement. Although there is no drum in *San Salvador,* the men appear to be playing capoeira – and not a type of war dance – as we can see the man in the center preparing to go down on what seems to be a *negativa,* while two fighters play "against" each other. The movement of the player wearing a hat has many similarities with the one depicted in *Jogar Capoëra;* on the far left of the image, we can see that a man is kissing a woman and neither are paying attention to the game, while the other three people appear to be watching the *capoeiristas.*

There are several elements of capoeira as depicted by most painters of the early nineteenth century. For instance, consider the "air of cheerfulness" among the seven people who are standing or playing, while a couple seems to be relaxed, watching the *capoeiristas* as captured by Rugendas. A "war dance" would not be the most appropriate interpretation of the image, but rather a dance-fighting-game taking place among four players, as in the early nineteenth century there were no rules to discipline the practice and tell people how they could or could not celebrate an event, invoke their African ancestral cultures, or simply express happiness.

## *Negroes Fighting*

Augustus Earle's watercolor *Negroes Fighting, Brazils* (ca. 1822), shows two men playing capoeira in one of the oldest visual documents of the art. One man

---

\**Malerische Reise in Brasilien.* Part I, plate 27.

appears to be striking the other with a *benção,* the front heel kick, which is perhaps the simplest of all capoeira moves.

## "Convoi funèbre d'un fils de roi nègre"

This other beautiful image by Jean Baptiste Debret, also from *Voyage pittoresque et historique au Brésil*, depicts a "Funeral Procession of a Son of a Black King," showing one of the participants apparently performing a cartwheel, an element that would later be incorporated into capoeira under the term *aú*.\* Nestor Capoeira, one of the greatest contributors to the documented history of capoeira, states that the *aú* was not present in the capoeira of the 1800s in Rio de Janeiro. In fact, I believe this move was imported from European acrobatic and circus traditions – as we explored earlier – in the late nineteenth century (or perhaps early twentieth century) directly to Rio de Janeiro, the most important urban center in that period, before it reached Bahia during the constant cultural exchanges between the two regions.

## O Calço ou a Rasteira

All this invaluable nineteenth century visual information, plus the early twentieth-century accounts – including illustrations such as the ones from the cartoonist Kalixto for the Brazilian magazine Kosmos – in 1906 (one of which can be seen in the opening to this chapter), can be fairly suggestive of the main, or basic moves used by the *capoeiristas* of the different eras.\*\*

In the Kalixto image that opens this chapter, for instance, the man on the ground is performing a *negativa,* just after having swept his opponent off

---

\**Voyage pittoresque et historique au Brésil*. Plate 16.
\*\*KALIXTO (Rio de Janeiro, 1906) O Calço ou a Rasteira, *KOSMOS, Revista Artística, Científica e Literária*, Rua da Assembléia, n. 62, Rio de Janeiro. Ano III, 1906, n. 3, Março. Mensal.

his feet, perhaps using a *calço* (a hitting wedge). It was common during the early years of the twentieth century for an experienced *capoeirista*, and for those who considered themselves as true *malandros*, to wear their best suits, often white ones, including hats and handkerchief. The saying is that the good *capoeirista* (or *malandro*) could play capoeira and not dirty his clothes.

## Razor, Handkerchief and Prestige in Capoeira

Some *capoeiristas* of that time went a little too far, and exhibited themselves in a contest where a banknote was put on the ground, in the center of the ring formed by other *capoeiristas* and the general public, in the streets of Rio. The one who caught the bill in his mouth (without the help of his adversary) was the winner – both of the game and of the money!

According to Pedro Abib, the razor was once a widely used weapon by the *capoeiristas*, most probably a legacy of the Portuguese, who had introduced it among the *capoeiristas* in Rio de Janeiro back in the nineteenth century, as Abib explains:*

> *The Portuguese "singers of Fado," mainly from the city of Lisbon, who used to hang out in the traditional neighborhoods of Alfama, Mouraria and Madragoa at the beginning of the twentieth century, were socially very close to the capoeiras of Rio de Janeiro; besides attending to the same environments: ports, bohemia, brothels, bars, they were also considered marginal people who suffered severe persecution from the police, as the capoeiras around here. And in these conflicts with the police, and also in disputes between their peers, the razor was a weapon that was always available, and was often responsible for severe injuries among them, even death in many cases.*

---

*Pedro Abib published the books *Capoeira Angola, Cultura Popular e o Jogo dos Saberes na Roda* (2005) and *Mestres e Capoeiras Famosos da Bahia* (2009).

*Even the "silk scarf" worn on the neck, indispensable part of the old time classic capoeira (and of the samba) clothing – those who wore traditional hats, white suits, two-color shoes and a ring in the left ear – had a very specific function: to protect themselves against the sharp blow of the razor. The "esguião," as the silk scarf was also known, had the property to prevent the cut from the sharpest razor, because the silk made the razor glide over the surface without reaching the victim's neck.*[134]

In these delicious passages below, from Gilberto Freyre and Elísio de Araújo, the intolerance – both of the Arab and the Negoes in Rio de Janeiro – can be observed in its entirety:

*If they were complaining about them to the police of the Prince Regent, as if they were disturbing dancers, the English and French, who did not see with good eyes either the Arab windows able to hide thieves or the capoeira experts in head butts and wheel kicks, must have regretted some of their complaints.*

*In the study already cited, Elísio de Araújo stresses that, from 1814 "there is a gradual and frightful increase of the aggressive search actions against individuals found in possession of a razor, or accused of inflicting wounds made by these weapons," which seems to indicate that, only in the face of the brutal police pursuit that was developed after 1808 against them, as well as against the Arab windows and their oriental roofs, the African drumming and medicine and – by reason or under always the same pretext: to avoid such Orientalisms and Africanisms in the eyes, ears and taste, if not also in the interests of the "perfectly civilized" Europeans, that is, the ones from Northern Europe – the capoeiras have resorted to the razor and the knife as weapons of defense against the police, and even of aggression against intolerant whites. These actions deserve detailed study because they project – according to Araújo – "intense light on the whole of the exercises that constitute the practice of capoeira, from which perhaps the leading one was the so called "head butt"*[135]

From the top of our twenty-first century, in accessing police reports from Rio and Bahia, we can observe that there was an important transition between the practice of capoeira reported in 1770, in the nineteenth century and in the early twentieth century, including its important social and racial reflexes, and we can compare them to the practice of the sport after the 1960s, the golden age of capoeira, perhaps the frontier that was waiting to be surmounted. And capoeira did go beyond.

We have seen throughout this book that capoeira is the product of its own diasporic experience, a branch of a large tree that grew into a unique and complex social art – which cannot be dissociated from its historical and anthropological perspectives.

## An Urban and European Blend

During the late eighteenth and early nineteenth centuries, capoeira migrated from rural areas to the more populated urban centers – especially to Rio de Janeiro, the capital of Brazil and the busiest port of entry for people and new cultures coming from Europe, and where capoeira's original and fighting characteristics underwent important changes with the infamous *maltas* and the use of the Portuguese "razor heritage" that we have just seen. These gangs of street toughs often challenged other enemy *maltas* and the political order in Rio de Janeiro. This triggered the special Decree 847 issued on November 15, 1889, which prohibited the practice of capoeira in the national territory of Brazil. This prohibition continued until President Getúlio Vargas decriminalized capoeira in 1937 and subsequently recognized it in 1953 as "the only genuine national sport."

In the mid-twentieth century, the original capoeira from Bahia was already established in Rio de Janeiro, together with its idiosyncrasies, and continued to develop under new influences. At first, these new influences came from the urban marginalized people – with still a trace of the old *maltas* – who used capoeira as a means of social and physical survival. Then capoeira started to spread among the street gangs and the poor people of the *favelas* and the *morros*, where many capoeira schools survived with the help of students coming from the educated middle and upper classes. This moment was paramount for the development of capoeira from a marginalized practice to a socially palatable sport, or from an exclusive cultural and more rudimentary perspective to a more developed physical art.

In this vein, who were, then, the main "players" during the transition from the Golden Age of capoeira to the present day?

## The Schools That Changed the World

It would be impossible, in this book, to list and comment all the important *capoeiristas* and *mestres* who contributed to capoeira from the early nineteenth century to the present day. I lack both space and the ability to do them all justice – for which I apologize. However, two groups stand out as pioneers of the new scale that rates capoeira among one of the most practiced fighting-sports in over 150 countries:

### *The Golden Age of Capoeira*

There is a typical Bahian dish that my mother used to make called *vatapá*. Everyone knew that hers was the best ever made (I am glad that my wife and I have the original recipe today!). She learned from her former *baiana* nanny when she was just 15 years old in the city of Vitória, Espírito Santo, where they are famous for perhaps the best *moqueca de peixe* (typical fish stew) in the world. Her nanny, born as a slave in Bahia in 1868, had learned from her mother, a former slave of the *casa grande* in Bahia, which borders the state of Espírito Santo. It was a wonderful mixture of cultures! This *vatapá* made many people happy in Rio de Janeiro, especially in the Ipanema of the 1960s, during my father's receptions of his fellow American colleagues.

I see capoeira from Bahia and Rio de Janeiro just like this *vatapá* and the other cultures discussed earlier: a delicious blend from its origin in mysterious, culturally exotic and beautiful Bahia to its assimilation and further development in agitated, culturally complex, yet also beautiful urban Rio de Janeiro.

In the 1960s, what I call "the Golden Age of capoeira," several capoeira schools were established in Rio de Janeiro, and the art again boomed in Bahia – where its traditional form had survived – with some *mestres* and *capoeiristas* coming to teach the educated middle and upper-class students in Rio. Many of these students from Rio de Janeiro had migrated to Bahia during that decade to learn the Capoeira Regional of (and with) Mestre Bimba. In this same decade and the next, *mestres* from Bahia would bring and help spread modern capoeira throughout the other states of Brazil.

This important migration period "from-to-from Rio and Bahia," in an ample sense, had, among many important actors in Rio de Janeiro, three who deserve special reverence for the origins and scope of their influence: the Senzala School of Capoeira, with most of its *mestres* coming from Bahia and Rio de Janeiro; ABADÁ Capoeira, with its gestation in the folkloric group Olodumaré – later called Brasil Tropical – with the spectacle "Furacões da Bahia" (Bahia's Hurricanes), which took capoeira, among other Afro-traditions, to other countries in South America and to Europe (and the birth of ABADÁ from within the Senzala school); and the Grupo Folclórico da Bahia (Folkloric Group of Bahia), with their show "Vem Camará," presented in Rio de Janeiro in 1966. Their brief history told in these pages will not do justice to the many other important *mestres* who were both an inspiration and the founders of Brazil's unique culture.

In a breakthrough for the middle and upper classes, the young Senzala "red cords" would continue to practice in Bahia with Bimba, Pastinha, and in the *rodas* of Waldemar da Paixão and Traíra during the 1960s. In Rio, the proximity with the samba schools of masters Leopoldina, Artur Emidio and Roque helped bridge different cultures in the rich city's cultural scenario.

The Senzala Group is one of the most representative groups of capoeira in the world, and, as of the time these words were written, it has been established throughout Brazil, in several countries in Europe, and in the United States.

Mestre Gato kindly updated me on the 18 red cords who helped make the history of Senzala and later left the group for different reasons: Rafael, Preguiça, Borracha, Mosquito (in memoriam), Nestor, Anzol, Bermuda, Paulinho, Negão Muzenza (in memoriam), Caio, Lua, Camisa, Claudio Moreno (in memoriam), Arara, Mula, Marron, Amendoin and Azeite (in memoriam).

Currently, the 18 red cords in activity are: Paulo Flores, Claudio Danadinho, Gato, Peixinho, Gil Velho, Garrincha, Sorriso, Itamar, Toni Vargas, Ramos, Elias, Beto, Feijão, Samara, Arruda, Abutre, Zumbi and Irandir.

The Grupo Folclórico da Bahia (Folkloric Group of Bahia), directed by legendary Mestre Acordeon, brought important *capoeiristas* with their show "Vem Camará," presented in Rio de Janeiro in 1966, including Camisa Roxa and Preguiça. While in Rio, Acordeon left his impression on the young Senzala members, teaching them some new techniques. When the group left Rio, Preguiça decided to stay to join Senzala as one of their historic masters.

ABADÁ-Capoeira was founded in 1988 by Mestre Camisa, who was introduced to Senzala in 1972 by his famous brother, Camisa Roxa, during their tour with the show "Furacões da Bahia," organized by Camisa Roxa. Over time, Camisa created his own style, developed a new cord system and became the leader of the largest capoeira organization in the world, with more than 40 thousand members in 30 countries and in every state of Brazil.

Currently ABADÁ has two Gran-Mestres (white cord), Camisa and Camisa Roxa; and two Mestres, Nagô and Cobra (red-white cord).

Capoeira Brasil was founded in 1989, in Rio de Janeiro, by Mestres Boneco, Paulão, and Paulinho Sabiá (black cords, in their system), who had studied at Senzala. The group grew to be perhaps the second largest capoeira organizations in the world, with branches spread throughout Brazil, as well as in Africa, Asia, Europe, Oceania, and North and South America.

Developed as a legitimate representative of the old capoeira of Rio de Janeiro – a legacy from the old street meetings of the central and north zones of Rio – Grupo Muzenza (with the white cord as the highest graduation) was founded in 1972 by Mestre Paulão, who used to enjoy some *rodas* at Senzala (despite not being a member of the group), and was established in the city of Curitiba, in southern Brazil, by Mestre Burguês, the present-day head of the group.

## *Early Contributions*

Other groups and individuals also contributed to the development of capoeira in Brazil, but, in their majority, these groups, as well as the "old masters" of modern capoeira, contributed to the preservation and dissemination of the "capoeira culture," while Senzala, besides learning and preserving the cultural factor, went beyond and also brought a continued development of the "physical art" of capoeira. The famous Senzala Saturday *rodas,* held at the Associação dos Servidores Civis do Brasil (the Brazilian Association of Civil Servants), were decisive factors for the technical changes that would occur in the development of the art in the following years in Brazil. The "open doors" to guests from all origins, to new groups and masters and to families and friends, where everyone was welcome in a nice friendly environment, were an important part of the determining factors of "the golden age of capoeira" in a predominant way.

Capoeira in Rio had acquired an unusual style, mostly due to its unique, diversified urban-cultural heritage – this *vatapá* blend, which was very much attached to Bahia in the late nineteenth and early twentieth centuries, yet with some new ingredients.

One of the most important and legitimate representatives of the Bahian capoeira in the suburbs of Rio de Janeiro in the 1950s and early 1960s was the Angola São Bento Pequeno school of capoeira, founded by Mestre Paraná in

Bonsucesso, who would at times play his perfect *berimbau* with Mestre Artur Emidio, who had a school in Higienópolis, and in his famous *rodas de capoeira* in Bonsucesso on Sundays. Emídio was considered by some *capoeiristas* as the first true Bahian representative of capoeira to organize classes in Rio de Janeiro in the early 1950s without the official label of "Regional" or "Angola," but rather just "plain capoeira leaned in Itabuna, Bahia" – before coming to Rio, but without the *pancadaria*, the brawl Emídio once categorized as "Capoeira de Sinhô" played in the rich middle and upper class south zone of Rio at the time. And there was also Mestre Mario Santos, of the school of capoeira and folk group Bonfim, in Olaria, and, of course, Mestre Roque, from Grupo Bantus de Capoeira of the *favela* of Pavão e Pavãozinho, which borders the neighborhoods of Ipanema and Copacabana. If we could identify the "missing link" of the late-nineteenth-century capoeira with what I call the "Golden Age" of the 1960s and beyond, these schools and masters (among others not mentioned here, though never forgotten) would have to be remembered.

The *capoeira de sinhô* was taught from the 1930s to the 1950s in Ipanema by Mestre Sinhozinho. Some say it was a rather unique "Capoeira Carioca" (from Rio), without music, more dedicated to the fighting aspects, a "street-fight capoeira," which may have generated some of the moves that are related to the capoeira played in Rio de Janeiro, such as the *compasso* (which was called *meia-lua de compasso* at the Grupo Bantus in Rio). However, despite its contribution to the martial art of capoeira, many *capoeiristas* from the Regional style created by Mestre Bimba contest its genuine capoeira provenance.

# Capoeira Angola

Capoeira Angola is a multicultural manifestation. It encompasses Afro-Brazilian ritualistic elements, dance, fight and musical performance – including that of exotic instruments. It is a system of personal defense and at the same time a ludic form of entertainment, where two "players" pretend to outmaneuver each other in the game of capoeira, using finesse, slyness and deception inside the *roda*.

The main objective is to find a way for an implied strike during the *jogo*, rendering the partner-opponent defenseless or dominated by the (temporary) superiority of the other *capoeirista*. It differs from Capoeira Regional partly in its objective and aggressiveness, thus in the martial arts aspects of capoeira.

## Mestre Pastinha

In 1941 Vicente Ferreira Pastinha, known as Mestre Pastinha, founded the first officially recognized school of what he called Capoeira Angola, the "Centro Esportivo de Capoeira Angola." His purpose was to preserve the traditional capoeira from the old slaves of Bahia, which could still be performed without relying mainly on martial arts elements, in an attempt to differentiate "original" capoeira from the Capoeira Regional that was created by Mestre Bimba in the 1930s.

## Capoeira Regional

Capoeira Regional is a newer form of Capoeira developed by Mestre Bimba in the early twentieth century in order to popularize capoeira, which was strongly associated with the criminal elements of Brazil. Capoeira Regional has most of the basic techniques of Capoeira Angola plus traumatic moves and takedowns, and is generally more athletic and more devoted to the martial arts aspects of the art, while maintaining the ludic ones.

In the early 1970s, a few *mestres* and *capoeiristas* of Capoeira Regional introduced a number of acrobatic jumps, back handsprings and jumping spinning kicks into their repertoire of moves, with which some rare purists still disagree.

The fact is that capoeira is still evolving, and, as in language, it is practically impossible to avoid such implementations brought to the *rodas* by enthusiastic students. Moreover, I have personally debated the matter with some of the most representative *mestres* of Capoeira Regional and of contemporary capoeira, who were unanimously in favor of these new implementations, "as long as they fit within the philosophy of the *jogo.*"

## Mestre Bimba

Manuel dos Reis Machado, known as Mestre Bimba, came into contact with Asian martial arts in Rio de Janeiro in the 1930s, where he incorporated new martial art elements and techniques to create his Capoeira Regional, in order to make it more attractive to youth and to the more educated classes.* However, all the elements of the capoeira we see today were present, inherited from ancient original African elements later developed into capoeira by the Afro-Brazilian experience. What Bimba did was help consolidate capoeira as a sport and create awareness of the fact that it was also a complex martial art.

Bimba's newer form of capoeira is now viewed as an efficient martial art and is often presented as a more athletic alternative to Mestre Pastinha's Capoeira Angola. Bimba is credited with having given capoeira the basis it needed to gain widespread international interest.

---

*Some old-time *capoeiristas* used to say that Bimba had also incorporated techniques from *batuque-boi,* or simply *batuque,* the fighting-dance seen earlier, and of which his father was known as a champion.

# Contemporary Capoeira

Nowadays we can see a renewed capoeira, one that is globalized and that maintains the old traditions while simultaneously offering the more modernized style of Regional and Angola. This perhaps has proved to be a great way to fraternize and retain comradeship amongst practitioners of all genders, ethnic origins, nationalities, ages and creeds – thanks to the living Mestres of Capoeira of all trends, who are those truly responsible for the development of millions of *capoeiristas* in more than 150 countries around the world. There is no doubt that the contributions to the art of capoeira made by Mestre Bimba and Mestre Pastinha laid the foundations for modern-day capoeira in Brazil and the world over, and also helped preserve its roots.

# CAPOEIRA MOVES & PHONOLOGY

*According to the IPA (International Phonetic Alphabet)*

| Move | Transcription | Move | Transcription |
|---|---|---|---|
| açoite de braço | [aˌsoytʃidʒiˈbrasu] | armada | [aRˈmada] |
| armada baixa | [aRˌmadaˈbayʃa] | armada dupla | [aRˌmadaˈdupla] |
| armada pulada | [aRˌmadapuˈlada] | arpão | [aRˈpãw] |
| arpão de cabeça | [aRˌpãwdʒicaˈbesa] | arrastão | [aRaʃˈtãw] |
| asfixiante | [aʃfiksiˈãtʃi] | aú | [aˈu] |
| aú agulha | [aˌuaˈguʎa] | aú alternado | [aˌuawteRˈnadu] |
| aú angola | [aˌuãˈgola] | aú batido | [aˌubaˈtʃidu] |
| aú batido de cotovelo | [aubaˌtʃidudʒikotoˈvelu] | aú batido duplo | [aubaˌtʃiduˈduplu] |
| aú com uma mão | [aˌucõumaˈmãw] | aú cortado | [aˌukoRˈtadu] |
| aú de costas | [aˌudʒiˈkoʃtaʃ] | aú de frente | [aˌudʒiˈfrẽtʃi] |

Photo-Art of Mestre Ricardo playing in a *roda* of Mestre Touro at the Bahia Festival held at Botafogo Club, Rio de Janeiro, in the 1970s.

| Move | Transcription | Move | Transcription |
|------|---------------|------|---------------|
| aú dobrado | [aˌudoˈbradu] | aú fechado | [aˌufeˈʃadu] |
| aú giratório | [aˌuʒiraˈtɔryu] | aú invertido | [aˌuĩveRˈtʃidu] |
| aú sem mãos | [aˌuˈsẽmãwʃ] | aú sem mãos reverso | [ausẽˌmãwʃReˈvɛRsu] |
| balanço | [baˈlãsu] | bananeira | [banaˈneyra] |
| banda | [ˈbãda] | banda de costas | [ˌbãdadʒiˈkɔʃtaʃ] |
| banda de dentro | [ˌbãdadʒiˈdẽtru] | benção | [ˈbẽsãw] |
| benção pulada | [ˌbẽsãwpuˈlada] | biriba | [biˈriba] |
| bloqueio | [bloˈkeyu] | bloqueio de dentro | [bloˌkeyudʒiˈdẽtru] |
| boca de calça | [ˌbokadʒiˈkawsa] | boca de calça de costas | [bokadʒiˌkawsadʒiˈkɔʃtaʃ] |
| borrão | [boˈRãw] | cabeçada | [kabeˈsada] |
| calcanheira | [kawkãˈɲeyra] | chapa | [ˈʃapa] |
| chapa baixa | [ˌʃapaˈbayʃa] | chapa de chão | [ˌʃapadʒiˈʃãw] |
| chapa de costas | [ˌʃapadʒiˈkɔʃtaʃ] | chapa de frente | [ˌʃapadʒiˈfrẽtʃi] |
| chapa giratória | [ˌʃapaʒiraˈtɔrya] | chapa lateral | [ˌʃapalateˈraw] |
| chapéu de couro | [ʃaˌpɛwdʒiˈkowru] | chibata | [ʃiˈbata] |
| cintura desprezada | [sĩˌturadeʃpreˈzada] | cocorinha | [kɔkɔˈriɲa] |
| coice de mula | [ˌkoysidʒiˈmula] | compasso | [kõˈpasu] |
| compasso pulado | [kõˌpasupuˈlado] | corta-capim | [ˌkɔRtakaˈpĩ] |
| cotovelada | [kotoveˈlada] | crucifixo | [krusiˈfiksu] |
| cruz | [ˈkruʃ] | cruzado | [kruˈzadu] |
| cutelo | [kuˈtɛlu] | dedeira | [deˈdeyra] |
| descida na negativa | [deˌsidananegaˈtʃiva] | entrada | [ẽˈtrada] |
| envergado | [ẽveRˈgadu] | escala | [eʃˈkala] |
| escorão | [eʃkoˈrãw] | escorpião | [eʃkoRpiˈãw] |
| escorumelo | [eʃkoruˈmɛlu] | esquiva | [eʃˈkiva] |
| esquiva baixa | [eʃˌkivaˈbayʃa] | esquiva de frente | [eʃˌkivadʒiˈfrẽtʃi] |
| esquiva lateral | [eʃˌkivalateˈraw] | folha seca | [ˌfoʎaˈseka] |
| folha seca invertida | [foʎaˌsekaĩveRˈtʃida] | folha seca lateral | [foʎaˌsekalateˈraw] |
| folha seca parafuso | [foʎaˌsekaparaˈfuzu] | gafanhoto | [gafaˈɲotu] |
| galopante | [galoˈpãtʃi] | gancho | [ˈgãʃu] |
| ginga | [ˈʒĩga] | giro | [ˈʒiru] |
| godeme | [goˈdemi] | helicóptero | [eliˈkɔpteru] |
| joelhada | [ʒoeˈʎada] | macaco | [maˈkaku] |
| macaco baixo | [maˌkakuˈbayʃu] | macaco baixo lateral | [makakuˌbayʃulateˈraw] |
| macaco de chão | [maˌkakudʒiˈʃãw] | macaco em pé | [maˌkakuẽˈpɛ] |
| macaco lateral | [maˌkakulateˈraw] | macaco reverso | [maˌkakuReˈvɛRsu] |
| mariposa | [mariˈpoza] | martelo | [maRˈtɛlu] |

| Move | Transcription | Move | Transcription |
|------|---------------|------|---------------|
| martelo cruzado | [maR‚tɛlukru'zadu] | martelo preso | [maR‚tɛlu'prezu] |
| martelo pulado | [maR‚tɛlupu'ladu] | martelo rodado | [maR‚tɛluRo'dadu] |
| martelo rodado voador | [maRtɛluRo‚daduvoa'doR] | meia-lua de chão | [meya‚luadʒi'ʃãw] |
| meia-lua de compasso | [meya‚luadʒikõ'pasu] | meia-lua de frente | [meya‚luadʒi'frētʃi] |
| meia-lua presa | [meya‚lua'preza] | meia-lua pulada | [meya‚luapu'lada] |
| meia-lua reversão | [meya‚luaRever'sãw] | meia-lua solta | [meya‚lua'sowta] |
| mola | ['mɔla] | mortal | [moR'taw] |
| mortal de costas | [moR‚tawdʒi'kɔʃtaʃ] | mortal de frente | [moR‚tawdʒi'frētʃi] |
| negativa | [nega'tʃiva] | negativa angola | [nega‚tʃivã'gɔla] |
| negativa de frente | [nega‚tʃivadʒi'frētʃi] | negativa derrubando | [nega‚tʃivadeRu'bãdu] |
| negativa escala | [nega‚tʃivaeʃ'kala] | negativa lateral | [nega‚tʃivalate'raw] |
| negativa tesoura | [nega‚tʃiva'tezowra] | parafuso | [para'fuzu] |
| passa-pé | [pasa'pɛ] | pião de cabeça | [pi‚ãwdʒica'besa] |
| pisão | [pi'zãw] | ponte | ['põtʃi] |
| ponteira | [põ'teyra] | ponteira alta | [põ‚teyra'awta] |
| ponteira baixa | [põ‚teyra'bayʃa] | ponteira lateral | [põ‚teyralate'raw] |
| ponteira média | [põ‚teyra'mɛdya] | ponteira pulada | [põ‚teyrapu'lada] |
| prancha | ['prãʃa] | prancha reversa | [‚prãʃaRe'vɛRsa] |
| pulo do gato | [‚puludu'gatu] | pulo do macaco | [‚puluduma'kaku] |
| queda de esquiva | [‚kɛdadʒieʃ'kiva] | queda de lado | [‚kɛdadʒi'ladu] |
| queda de quatro | [‚kɛdadʒi'kwatru] | queda de rim | [‚kɛdadʒi'Rĩ] |
| queda de três | [‚kɛdadʒi'treʃ] | queixada | [key'ʃada] |
| queixada de frente | [key‚ʃadadʒi'frētʃi] | rabo de arraia | [‚Rabudʒia'Raya] |
| raiz | [Ra'iʃ] | rasteira | [Raʃ'teyra] |
| rasteira de chão | [Raʃ‚teyradʒi'ʃãw] | rasteira de costas | [Raʃ‚teyradʒi'kɔʃtaʃ] |
| rasteira de mão | [Raʃ‚teyradʒi'mãw] | rasteira em pé | [Raʃ‚teyraē'pɛ] |
| rasteira giratória | [Raʃ‚teyraʒira'tɔrya] | relógio | [Re'lɔʒyu] |
| resistência | [Reziʃ'tēsya] | rolê | [Ro'le] |
| s-dobrado | [ɛsido'bradu] | salto | ['sawtu] |
| suicídio | [suy'sidyu] | telefone | [tele'foni] |
| tesoura | [te'zowra] | tesoura angola | [te‚zowrã'gɔla] |
| tesoura de frente | [te‚zowradʒi'frētʃi] | tombo da ladeira | [‚tõbudala'deyra] |
| troca | ['trɔka] | troca de negativa | [‚trɔkadʒinega'tʃiva] |
| vingativa | [vĩga'tʃiva] | volta por cima | [‚vowtapoR'sima] |
| vôo do morcego | [‚voudumoR'segu] | xangô | [ʃã'go] |
| xangô de frente | [ʃã‚godʒi'frētʃi] | | |

# GLOSSARY OF YORÙBÁ WORDS

| Yorùbá Name | Meaning |
| --- | --- |
| Adágún Léwà | Beautiful Lagoon. |
| aginiṣọ | A giant snail. The worshipers of Ọ̀ṣun are forbidden to say the word "ìgbín" (see the glossary entry for that word). |
| àkóso | Government, administration. |
| àlàáfíà | Peace. |
| alajapa | Traders of fruits and medicinal herbs. |
| alaso | Traders of cloth. |
| aso-oke | A top cloth. A generally colorful hand-loomed fabric worn by men and women. |

Yorùbá Mask from West Africa (c) Copyright Horsham District Council (1991).

| Yorùbá Name | Meaning |
| --- | --- |
| efo tete | Amaranthus. |
| egbe | Guild. |
| elepe | Traders of oil. |
| ìbárẹ́ | Harmony, friendship. |
| ìgbín | A Nigerian giant snail. |
| igi ópẹ | A palm tree, the "dendezeiro." |
| Ìlàjú | City. |
| irun orí | Hair styles. |
| irungígẹ́ | Hair beadmaking. |
| ọ́rọ́ọlá | Wealth. |
| Odù Ifá | The 256 chapters (Odù) of the Ifá system of divination.* |
| Odùduwà | The ancestor of all crowned Yorùbá kings. |
| Ògún | The òrìsà who controls the fire and the making of iron artifacts, war, craftsmanship and inventions. |
| Olódùmarè | Ọlọrun. The creator of the universe. |
| Olúfón | Obàtálá. The first òrìsà created by Olódùmarè. |
| òrìsà | One of the spirits who represent the forces of nature, reflecting one of the manifestations of Olódùmarè. |
| ọgbọ́n | Knowledge. |
| ọkọ̀ | Boat. |
| Ọmọ Ọba | Prince. |

*The Ifá Divination system was added in 2005 by UNESCO to its list of "Masterpieces of the Oral and Intangible Heritage of Humanity." Source: http://www.unesco.org/

# NOTES

1   FISKE, John (1892). *The Discovery of America: With Some Account of Ancient America and The Spanish Conquest*, pp. 372.

2   SMALLWOOD, Stephanie E. (2007). *Saltwater Slavery: A Middle Passage from Africa to American Diaspora*, pp. 15.

3   MINAHAN, James (2002). *Encyclopedia of the Stateless Nations*, pp. 225.

4   SHERWOOD (2005), http://www.edithsherwood.com/marchionni_afro_portuguese_ivories/index.php.

5   FREY, Sylvia R. and WOODY, Betty (1999). *Slavery to Emancipation in the Atlantic World*, pp. 9.

6   Ibid.

7   DIFFIE, Bailey Wallys and WINIUS, George Davison (1977). *Foundations of the Portuguese Empire, 1415–1580*, pp. 150.

8   RICH , Edwin Ernest RICH and WILSON , C. H. (1967). *The Economy of Expanding Europe in the Sixteenth and Seventeenth Centuries.*

9   MONTE, Mayombe Palo and CABRERA, Lydia (1986). *Reglas de Congo*, pp. 93.

10  *The Autobiography of a Runaway Slave* (1968/1994), pp. 31.

11  SUBLETTE, Ned (2007). *Cuba and its Music: From the First Drums to the Mambo, Volume 1*, pp. 268.

12  FONER , Laura and GENOVESE, Eugene D. (1969). *Slavery in the New World: A Reader in Comparative History*, pp. 211.

13  OLMOS, Margarite Fernández and GEBERT, Lizabeth Paravisini (2003). *Creole Religions of the Caribbean: An Introduction from Vodou and Santería to Obeah and Espiritismo*, pp. 132.

14  ELTIS,David (2000). *The Rise of African Slavery in the Americas*, pp. 255.

15  OLIVER, Paul (1971). *Shelter in Africa*, pp. 37.

16  GRANT, J. Andrew and SÖDERBAUM, Fredrik (2003).*The New Regionalism in Africa*, pp. 60.

17  SARTRE, Jean-Paul (1949). *Les Temps Modernes: Revue Mensuelle, Issues 48-53*, pp. 1395.

18  KLEIN, Herbert S. (1988). *African slavery in Latin America and the Caribbean*, pp. 181.

19  *The French Slave Trade: An Overview, in William and Mary Quarterly, Third Series, Vol. 58, No. 1,* New Perspectives on the Transatlantic Slave Trade (Jan., 2001), pp. 132.

20  HERSKOVITS, Melville J. (1941). *The Myth of the Negro Past*, pp. 16.

21  TAYLOR, Patrick (2001). *Nation Dance: Religion, Identity, and Cultural Difference in the Caribbean*, pp. 35.

22  BLUMBERG, Rhoda Lois (1971). *Black Life and Culture in the United States*, pp. 60.

23  OLMOS, Margarite Fernández and GEBERT, Lizabeth Paravisini (2003).*Creole Religions of the Caribbean: An Introduction from Vodou and Santería to Obeah and Espiritismo*, pp. 131.

24  RODRIGUEZ, Junius P. (2007). *The Historical Encyclopedia of World Slavery, Volume 1*, pp. 87.

25  Ibid., *Volume 2*, pp. 193.

26  ZINN, Howard (2006). *A people's History of the United States: 1492–present*, pp. 23.

27  *Ibid*, pp. 24.

28  LIVINGSTONE, David and LIVINGSTONE, Charles (1866). *Narrative of an Expedition to the Zambesi and its Tributaries*, pp. 4.

29  Ibid., pp. 136.

30  Ibid., pp. 537.

31  *Ibid*.

32  RODRIGUEZ, Junius P. (2007). *The Historical Encyclopedia of World Slavery, Volume 1*, pp. 624.

33  SELLSTRÖM, Tor (1999). *Sweden and National Liberation in Southern Africa: Volume 1*, pp. 58.

34  ATKINS, John (1735). *A Voyage to Guinea, Brazil and the West Indies; In His Majesty's Ships; the Swallow and the Weymouth*, pp. 53.

35  DAVENPORT, Frances Gardiner AND PAULLIN, Charles Oscar (1917). *Translation from European Treaties Bearing on the History of the United States and Its Dependencies to 1648*, pp. 23.

36  FREEMAN, Frederick (1838). *A Plea for Africa: Being Familiar Conversations on the Subject of Slavery and Colonization*, Third Edition, United States, pp. 59.

37    DAMES, Longworth and SEEMANN, E. (1903). *Folklore of the Azores*, Great Britain, pp. 125.

38    FONSECA, Homero. http://www.interblogs.com.br/homerofonseca/ Last visited September 2009.

39    COUTO, Jorge (1995). *A Construção do Brasil: Ameríndios, Portugueses e Africanos, do Início do Povoamento a Finais de Quinhentos,* Portugal, pp. 151.

40    DOMINGUES, Petrônio (2003). *Uma Historia Não Contada: Negro, Racismo e Branqueamento em São Paulo,* pp. 313.

41    Ibid., pp. 313.

42    ATKINS, John (1735). *A Voyage to Guinea, Brazil and the West Indies; In His Majesty's Ships; the Swallow and the Weymouth,* pp. 171.

43    FALCONBRIDGE, Alexander (1788). *An account of the slave trade on the coast of Africa,* pp. 17.

44    Ibid., pp. 18.

45    Ibid., pp. 13.

46    Ibid., pp. 14.

47    ANDERSON III, Robert Nelson (1996). *The Quilombo of Palmares: A New Overview of a Maroon State in Seventeenth-Century Brazil,* article, United States.

48    House of Commons (1853). *Parliamentary papers,* Volume 39, Parliament, London, Great Britain, pp. 209.

49    Ibid., pp. 208.

50    MARQUESE, Rafael de Bivar (2006). *The dynamics of slavery in Brazil: Resistance, the slave trade and manumission in the 17th to 19th centuries.* Novos Estudos – CEBRAP, São Paulo.

51    MARQUESE, Rafael de Bivar and PARRON, Tâmis Peixoto (2005). *Revista de História 152 – 1º,* pp. 123.

52    Ibid., pp. 122.

53    KARASCH, Mary C. (1972). *Slave Life in Rio de Janeiro, 1808–1850,* United States.

54    SOARES, Luís Carlos Soares (2007). *O "Povo de Cam" na Capital do Brasil: A Escravidão Urbana no Rio de Janeiro do Século IX,* Rio de Janeiro, pp. 89.

55    *The Journal of Latrobe* (1905). Volume 178, New York, pp. 180-181.

56    DUNHAM, Katherine (1969). *Island Possessed,* New York, pp. 280.

57    FLEURANT, Gerdès (1996). *Dancing Spirits: Rhythms and Rituals of Haitian Vodun, the Rada Rite,* United States, pp. 25-27.

58    BEHANZIN, Yolande and NÖEL, Joseph (2001). In *Doudou Diène from Chains to Bonds: The Slave Trade Revisited,* United States, pp. 334.

59   MÉRY, Moreau de Saint (2003). *In Maureen Warner Lewis, Central Africa in the Caribbean: Transcending Time, Transforming Culture,* Canada, pp. 236-237.

60   PLASTOW, Jane (1996). *African theatre and politics: the evolution of theatre in Ethiopia, Tanzania and Zimbabwe,* The Netherlands, pp. 22.

61   ATKINS, John (1735). *A Voyage to Guinea, Brazil and the West Indies; In His Majesty's Ships; the Swallow and the Weymouth,* pp. 53.

62   MITCHELL, James Clyde (1959). *The Kalela dance; aspects of social relationships among urban Africans in Northern Rodhesia,* United Kingdom.

63   RANGER, Terence O. (1975). *Dance and Society in Eastern Africa, 1890–1970: the Beni ngoma,* United States.

64   RODRIGUEZ, Junius (1997). *The Historical Encyclopedia of World Slavery,* pp. 127.

65   CALLY, Sully (1990). *Musiques et danses afro-caraïbes: Martinique,* University of Texas, pp. 59.

66   DECORSE, Christopher R. (2001). *An archaeology of Elmina: Africans and Europeans on the Gold Coast, 1400–1900,* pp. 27.

67   HERSKOVITS, Melville J. (1941). *The Myth of the Negro Past,* pp. 10.

68   FERNANDES, Florestan (1965). *A Integração do Negro na Sociedade de Classes,* São Paulo, V II, pp. 293.

69   HERSKOVITS, Melville J. (1941). *The Myth of the Negro Past,* pp. 10.

70   EMBREE, Edwin R. (1941). In HERSKOVITS, Melville J., *The Myth of the Negro Past,* United States, pp. 5.

71   LARSON, Thomas J. (2004). *The great adventure: the University of California Southern Africa expedition of 1947–1948,* United States, pp. 211.

72   Ibid., pp. 217.

73   Ibid., pp. 199.

74   Ibid., pp. 218.

75   Ibid., pp. 218.

76   Ibid., pp. 219.

77   NAMPALA, Lovisa T. and SHIGWEDHA, Vilho (2006). *Aawambo kingdoms, history and cultural change,* Switzerland, pp. 144.

78   BECKER, Heike (2005). In ARNFRED, Signe, *Re-thinking sexualities in Africa,* Sweden, pp. 40.

79   CAPOEIRA, Nestor (1992), *Capoeira, Fundamentos da Malícia,* Brazil, pp. 40, in http://www.capoeira.bz/mestreacordeon/capoeira/history.html.

80   POH, Johann Baptist Emanuel (1832). *Reise im Innern von Brasilien: in den Jahren 1817–1821,* Vienna, pp. 85.

81 SAINT-HILAIRE, Auguste de (1830). *Voyage dans les Provinces de Rio de Janeiro et de Minas Geraes (Voyage to the Provinces of Rio de Janeiro and Minas Gerais, Volume II*, Paris, pp. 166.

82 Ibid., pp. 166.

83 Ibid., pp. 232.

84 KOSTER, Henry (1817). *Travels in Brazil in the Years from 1809 to 1815, Volume I*, Unites States, pp. 241.

85 CHAMBERLAIN, Herny (1822). *Vistas e Costumes de Cidade e Arredores do Rio de Janeiro em 1819–1820*, Rio de Janeiro, 1943, pp. 105; London, plate 4.

86 WALSH, Robert (1831). *Notices of Brazil in 1828 and 1829, Volume II*, United States, pp. 101.

87 Ibid., pp. 187.

88 WETHERELL, James (1860). *Stray Notes from Bahia: Being Extracts from Letters, &c., During a Residence of Fifteen Years,* Great Britain, pp. 106.

89 RIBEYROLLES, Charles (1859). *Brazil Pittoresco: Historia-Descripções-Viagens-Instutuições-Colonização, Tomo 1*, Rio de Janeiro, pp. 47.

90 MANN, Kristin in MANN, Kristin and BAY, Edna G. (2001). *Rethinking the African Diaspora: The Making of a Black Atlantic World in the Bight of Benin and Brazil*, Great Britain, pp. 9.

91 FALOLA, Toyin and CHILDS, Matt D. (2004). *The Yoruba Diaspora in the Atlantic World*, Unites States, pp. 238.

92 RODNEY, Walter in FAGE, J. D. (1975). GRAY, Richard and OLIVER, Roland Anthony. *The Cambridge history of Africa, Volume 4*, pp. 616.

93 Ibid., pp. 250.

94 GEGGUS, David (2001). "The French Slave Trade: An Overview," in *The William and Mary Quarterly, Third Series, Vol. 58, No. 1*, United States, pp. 132.

95 HRBEK, Ivan (1992). *Africa from the Seventh to the Eleventh Century*, Great Britain, 1992), pp. 261.

96 FALCONBRIDGE, Alexander (1788). *An account of the slave trade on the coast of Africa*, London, pp. 23.

97 AKINJOGBIN, I. (1972). In ANENE, Joseph C. and BROWN, Godfrey N., *Africa in the Nineteenth and Twentieth Centuries: A Handbook for Teachers and Students*, United States, pp. 255.

98 CHARNEY, Sappho (1996). In RING, Trudy, SALKIN, Robert M. and LA BODA, Sharon, *International Dictionary of Historic Places: Middle East and Africa*, United States, pp. 5.

99    OLMOS, Margarite Fernández and GEBERT, Lizabeth Paravisini (2003). *Creole religions of the Caribbean: an introduction from Vodou and Santería to Obeah and Espiritismo,* New York, pp. 14.

100  LEWIS, Maureen Warner (2003). *Central Africa in the Caribbean: Transcending Time, Transforming Cultures,* Canada, pp. 199.

101  DANIEL, Yvonne (2005). *Dancing Wisdom: Embodied Knowledge in Haitian Vodou, Cuban Yoruba, and Bahian Candomblé,* United States, pp. 287.

102  DODSON, Jualynne E. (2008). *Sacred spaces and Religious Traditions in Oriente Cuba,* United States, pp. 42 and 105.

103  HERSKOVITS, Melville and HERSKOVITS, Frances (1958). *Dahomean Narrative,* United States, pp. 167.

104  CODO, Bellarmin C. (2001). In DIÈNE, Doudou, *From Chains to Bonds: The Slave Trade Revisited,* United States, pp. 61-62.

105  http://www.afropop.org/ (2007), last visited in January, 2010.

106  KUBIK, Gerhard (1979). *Angolan Traits in Black Music, Games and Dances of Brazil: A Study of African Cultural Extensions Overseas,* United States, pp. 31.

107  GROPPER (1972). In GALM, Eric A., *Beyond the Roda: The Berimbau de Barriga in Brazilian Music and Culture,* United States, 2004, pp. 45.

108  CEZIMBRA, Eduardo (2006).

109  OMARI-TUNKARA, Mikelle Smith (2005). *Manipulating the sacred: Yorùbá art, ritual, and resistance in Brazilian Candomblé,* United States, pp. 14.

110  MERRELL, Floyd (1999). *Capoeira and Candomblé: conformity and resistance in Brazil,* Spain, pp. 126.

111  VIANNA, Hermano and CHASTEEN, John Charles (1999). *Mistério do samba,* United States, pp. 27-28.

112  Negro Dances (1941). *The Crisis,* March, pp 93.

113  ZAKHARIA, Fouad, *at al.* (2009). *Characterizing the admixed African ancestry of African Americans,* London.

114  FRYER, Peter (2000). *Rhythms of resistance: African musical heritage in Brazil,* London, pp. 137.

115  SANDOVAL, Alonso de (2008). *Treatise on Slavery, Book I,* United States, pp. 47.

116  MOLLIEN, Gaspard Théodore (1820). *Travels in the Interior of Africa in the Sources of the Senegal and Gambia,* London, pp. 56-57.

117  BALLA, Mark (2003). *Brazilian Portuguese,* Australia, pp. 113.

118  LANG, George (2000). *Entwisted Tongues: Comparative Creole Literatures,* Amsterdam, pp. 49-52.

119 KUBIK, Gerhard (1979). *Angolan traits in Black music, games and dances of Brazil: a study of African Cultural Extensions Overseas,* Lisbon, pp. 11.

120 SAINT-HILAIRE, Auguste de (1847). *Voyage aux Sources du Rio de S. Francisco et dans la Province de Goyaz, Volume 1,* Paris, pp. 46.

121 Ibid., pp. 203.

122 Ibid., pp. 60.

123 *Enciclopédia de Música Brasileira,* in LOPES, Nei (2005) Partido-Alto: samba de bamba, Rio de Janeiro, pp 24.

124 SALM, Steven J. and Falola, Toyn (2002). *Culture and Customs of Ghana,* United States, pp. 177.

125 ARAÚJO, Nelson de (1986). *Pequenos Mundos: O Recôncavo,* Bahia, pp. 77.

126 PAIM, Zilda (1999). *Relicário Popular,* pp. 17.

127 Ibid., pp. 19.

128 Prof. Romario Itacaré, Grupo Folclórico Luanda.

129 AMARAL, Francisco Pacífico do (Pernambuco, 1884/1974), *Escavações: fatos da história de Pernambuco,* Pernambuco, pp. 230

130 TEIXEIRA, João Gabriel L. C. (2003). *In Popular Music and Society, Volume 26,* Issue 1 February, pp. 31-36.

131 ALTMAN, Fábio and BONIFÁCIO, José (2004). *A arte da entrevista,* São Paulo, pp. 362.

132 CAVALCANTI, Nireu, Jornal do Brasil (November 15, 1999), *CRÔNICAS DO RIO COLONIAL,* Caderno B, pp.22 and ANRJ – Tribunal da Relação – códice 24, livro 10.

133 FREYRE, Gilberto (Rio de Janeiro, 1951), *Sobrados e Mucambos: Decadência do Patriarcado Rural e Desenvolvimento do Urbano,* pp. 877.

134 ABID, Pedro *(Pedrão de João Pequeno).* Professor at the Universidade Federal da Bahia (Federal University of Bahia), musician and *capoeirista,* graduated by Mestre João Pequeno de Pastinha. In *A Navalha na Capoeira* (November 15, 2009), Portalcapoeira.com.

135 FREYRE, Gilberto (Rio de Janeiro, 1951), *Sobrados e Mucambos: Decadência do Patriarcado Rural e Desenvolvimento do Urbano,* pp. 876-877.

136 These works are licensed under the Creative Commons cc by-sa License. To view a copy of this license, visit http://creativecommons.org/about/licenses/.

House of Slaves, "The Door of No Return" on Gorée Island, Senegal. Photo by
Galen R. Frysinge. Gorée Island is part of the UNESCO World Heritage List.

House of Slaves, "Window in the Cubicle" on Gorée Island, Senegal. Photo by Galen R. Frysinge. Gorée Island is part of the UNESCO World Heritage List. Cubicle where the slaves were held waiting for their transport to the Americas on slave ships. They were usually stripped naked and fed like animals on the ships, under appalling and unhygienic conditions. Often a quarter of the "cargo" would perish before reaching their destination.

Replica of a wind rose from one of the earliest European nautical charts. Illustration by Joaquim Alves Gaspar after a nautical chart by cartographer Jorge de Aguiar (1492).

Slave Market, Lagos, in the Algarve, Portugal. The first Portuguese slave traders brought slaves from Africa and the Atlantic islands to be sold as merchandise in the mid-fifteenth century. Photo taken by the author (2001).

Beauties of Africa! The baobab tree (*Adansonia digitata*). Picture taken at Tarangire National Park, Tanzania, 2008, by Yoky. The baobab was used by the African indigenous people for several purposes. The bark of the baobab is used for cloth and rope, the leaves for condiments and medicines, while the fruit is edible.[136]

Cape Coast Castle, Ghana, 1999. Photo courtesy of Michael Tuite (source: University of Virginia at http://hitchcock.itc.virginia.edu). President Barack Obama and Mrs. Michelle Obama and family visited this UNESCO World Heritage Site in July 2009. Built originally by the Swedish Africa Company as Fort Carolusborg, it was later part of the Danish Gold Coast before it became the headquarters of the British Gold Coast.

Painting of slaves in chains at the House of Slaves Museum. Photo by Galen R. Frysinger. The house of slaves was built in 1776 by Dutch slave traders, on Gorée Island, Senegal. It was the last slave house built on the island. The first ones date back to 1536 and were built by the Portuguese, who first explored the island in 1444.

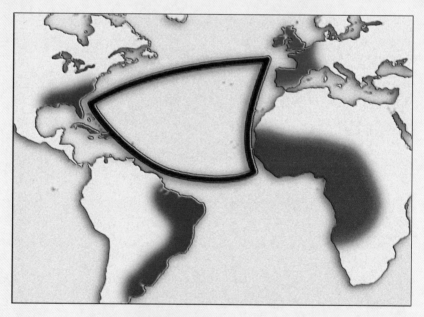

Triangular Slave Trade, The Middle Passage. Commercial goods from Europe were shipped to Africa for sale and trade for enslaved Africans. Africans were in turn brought to the regions depicted in blue, in what became known as the "Middle Passage." African slaves were thereafter traded for raw materials, which were returned to Europe to complete the "Triangular Trade." Illustration by Sémhur. Adapted map from a map by François Nancy, made for the UNESCO "The Slave Route" project.[136]

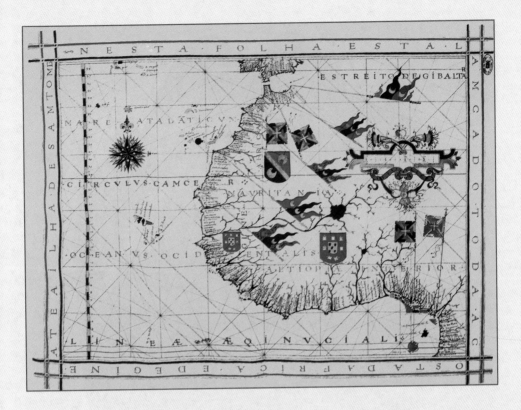

Nautical chart of a 1571 atlas, of Portuguese cartographer Fernão Vaz Dourado. Photo by Joaquim Alves Gaspar. The chart depicts the northwestern coast of Africa explored by Portuguese navigators, by order of Prince Henry the Navigator. (Portuguese National Archives of Torre do Tombo, Lisbon).

Two very similar Okhapo variety of Manillas from Nigeria. Manillas were a traditional West African copper currency, probably derived from original metal rings and bracelets used in ancient Africa and from the Yorùbá *mondua*. Earlier forms were made of copper, often horseshoe shaped with enlarged final terminations such as these. Manillas were a form of money in coastal Nigeria during the Atlantic slave trade. Photographer: Rosser1954 (2007).

Yorùbá Mask from West Africa © Copyright Horsham District Council. The Yorùbá people were one of the most influential and advanced societies in pre-colonial Africa, dominating several aspects of industrialization, cultural expressions and arts.

*A sleeping negro, Brazils* [ca. 1822]. Watercolor by Augustus Earle, 1793–1838. Kind courtesy of the National Library of Australia. Earle's works reflect the voyages he made around the world in the early nineteenth century. In April 1832 he embarked with Charles Darwin as topographical artist and draughtsman aboard the *Beagle*.

*Punishing negroes at Cathabouco, [i.e. Calabouco].* Rio de Janeiro [ca. 1822]. Watercolor by Augustus Earle, 1793–1838. Kind courtesy of the National Library of Australia.

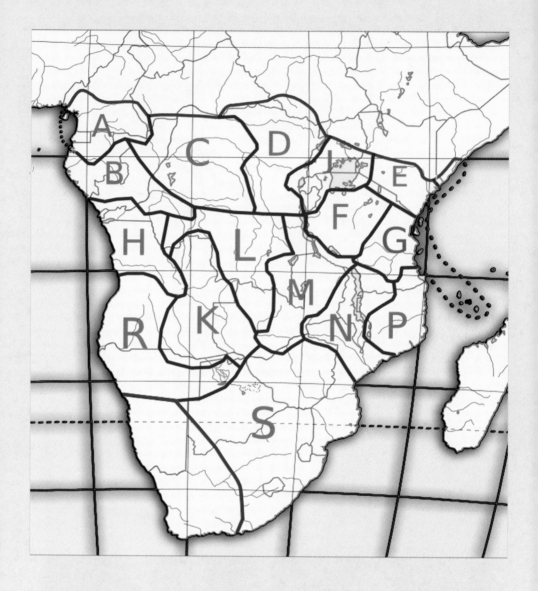

Classification of Geographic Bantu Zones by Malcolm Guthrie showing the
location of the sixteen Bantu-speaking zones of Africa. Besides the great ancient
Bantu migrations, Zone A – located mostly in present-day Cameroons – may
have been the "cultural intersection point" between the Yorùbá and the Bantu.
A reference for most scholars, Guthrie's works on the Bantu languages – *The
classification of the Bantu languages* (1948), London: Oxford University Press
for the International African Institute, and *Comparative Bantu: an introduction
to the comparative linguistics and prehistory of the Bantu languages* (1987-71), 4
vols. Farnborough: Gregg Press – are the most complete apporach to the Bantu
languages to date. Original illustration by Edricson (July 2007).[136]

*Arcos da Lapa* (Lapa Arches), Rio de Janeiro, Brazil – 2005. Oil painting by João Barcelos, contemporaneous artist whose figurative and impressionist (with an expressionist touch) works depict angles of traditional neighborhoods of Rio de Janeiro, eliminating traces of modernity that have interfered with the original landscape. Known as the cradle of bohemia in Rio, the Lapa neighborhood is also famous for its architecture, starting with the Arcos, which was an aqueduct built during the colonial period. Kind courtesy of João Barcelos.

*Negro fandango scene, Campo St. Anna, Rio de Janeiro* [ca. 1822]. Watercolor by Augustus Earle, 1793–1838. Kind courtesy of the National Library of Australia.

*Negroes Fighting, Brazils* [ca. 1822]. Watercolor by Augustus Earle, 1793–1838. Kind courtesy of the National Library of Australia. This impressive historic document shows what could be a capoeira *benção*, or one of its crescent kicks; the policeman exhibiting a repressive attitude depicts one of the earliest accounts of the police repression of capoeira.

The berimbau is the main instrument played in a capoeira roda. It consists of a wooden bow known as *verga* (a flexible stick), traditionally made from the *biriba* wood, which is native to Brazil. The musical bow is about 4 to 5 feet long (1.2 to 1.5 m), with a steel string (the *arame* – nowadays often taken from the inside of an automobile tire and earlier made from a variety of African vines) tightly strung and secured from one end of the *verga* to the other. A gourd (*cabaça*) resonator is attached to the lower portion of the *verga* by a loop of tough string. In the *roda*, one or more *berimbaus* (tipically up to three) are played with the help of a stick, called *vareta* or *baqueta*, a rattle, known as *caxixi*, and a coin (traditionally the *dobrão* – a Brazilian coin used in the eighteenth century during the reign of D. João V of Portugal), or a rather circular-shaped stone. The basic capoeira orchestra is generally completed with one *atabaque* (drum) and one or two *pandeiros* (tambourines).

Images kind courtesy of VirtualCapoeira (www.virtualcapoeira.com).

Yorùbá bronze head sculpture from the city of Ife, Nigeria c. 12ᵗʰ century.
Nigerian and Yorùbá arts are among the oldest in human history. Ife is an
ancient Yorùbá city, from which the deities Oduduwa and Obatala began the
creation of the world, under the command of the supreme deity Olodumare.
Photo by WaynaQhapaq (2007).

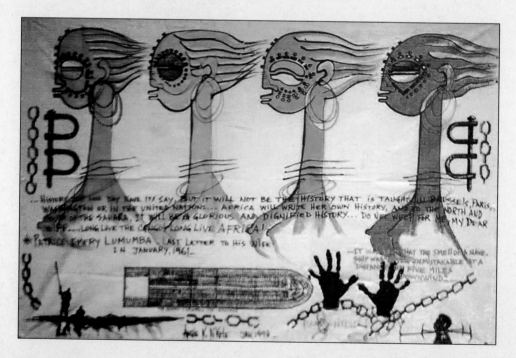

The Middle Passage. Drawing by Congo-born American artist Augie N'Kele,
executed with permanent markers on cloth. 1999. Kind courtesy of Augie N'Kele.